Dedicated to every Dad and Mum trying to do their best.

Thank you:

Amy, my love, for your support, and parenting wisdom.

Our kids, for bringing so much joy into our lives.

Mum and Dad for your love, encouragement, and wisdom.

Dave and Betsy for your love, generous hearts, and parenting guidance.

Claire, Olivia, Betsy, and Becky for the gift of your time and creativity
in laying out and editing BeTheDad.

And Betsy. Thank you for believing wholeheartedly
that the world needed BeTheDad. Here it is.

BE THE ~~MAN~~ DAD

Ferg Turnbull

Thank you for 'Be the Dad'.

Saved me, my relationship and my kids from
me losing my way as a man and a dad.

I have shared Be the Dad with so many people and hope it
impacts them in such a way as it did me.

I have embraced being a dad more than anything in the world and
I am happily expecting my 4th child. Something I would not have been
happy about a few years back before reading 'Be the Dad'.

Grateful to you and finding 'Be the Dad'.

BRETT
Queensland

2022 Copyright © Fergus Turnbull

Second print run 2023
ISBN 978-1-9911901-0-9
COL KINDLE

The Dad on the plane who needed a hand

"Hi I'm Ferg, that's my seat next to the window..... so what do you do?"

I was talking to a highly educated man on a flight home from Wellington to Christchurch in New Zealand. He was successful at his job, but was struggling in his personal and family life.

This dad needed some help.

I started passing on tips I have picked up in parenting my 5 kids, from books and wise parents. His face lit up as I passed on simple and practical ideas. As we landed, the air of helplessness that had surrounded him was replaced by a growing confidence and hope.

He was educated for his job but needed help in his marriage and parenting. If we study to be great dads and husbands like we train to be good at our jobs, we will get results far greater than our weekly paychecks.

I have written 'Be the Dad' for all the Dads (and Mums) who would like helpful and empowering tips to have great relationships with their spouse and children, and to enjoy living their lives.

I hope this book helps make your parenting adventure great.

Ferg

Family life

Marriage life

Personal life

BE THE ~~MAN~~ DAD

BE THE ~~MAN~~ DAD

Intro: What is 'Being the ~~Man~~ Dad'?

What is the difference between being 'The Man' and being 'The Dad'?

Being 'The Man' is aiming to be the guy who impresses others. Pulling off a great play in sports, saying something really funny or closing a great business deal. It feels good to earn respect and be 'The Man'.

Being 'The Dad' is being a great father to your family and making your family life as good as possible! It's being the guy that your kids look up to and model their lives off and the man your wife loves. Being 'The Dad' is finding fulfilment, healthiness and happiness in this busy work/parenting season of your life.

If being 'The Man' is impressing others, being 'The Dad' is embracing and enjoying your family life.

This book is about winning at being 'The Dad'. It is loaded with tips and 'how to's' to help you have a strong family and a great life. This book will help you find the time, joy and life balance to be that loving Dad for your kids and husband for your wife. You can get the best thoughts from a chapter in only 5-10 minutes. Read one chapter every couple of days and see how it positively impacts your parenting and family life. I know you will be encouraged and inspired.

You can read this book chronologically or pick and choose the chapters depending on what you need help with or want to learn about. Pace yourself, work on a couple of suggestions at a time and remember 'good things take time'.

Tried and true. I have written this book over 4 years through the birth of a fifth child and the death of my wife's cherished mother. As I reread the 'Be the Dad' final edit I am still being blessed by the lessons in these pages that are helping and encouraging me in my parenting now.

So go for it! Be 'The Dad' or 'The Mum' and take loving life to the next level for you and your family. And remember - to be loved by your Dad is one of the greatest experiences people can have in life.

Ferg

P.S. I am writing as a married dad so there will be heaps of references to being married and 'your wife'. Feel free to insert 'Be the Mum'.

Family life

1.

Be the 'Famous in your Family' Dad

Finding your life's meaning.
True significance is being highly esteemed
by those closest to you.

What is the purpose of my life?

Have you ever woken up and thought, what is my life about? You open up your phone and see someone with a worldwide following on social media rallying people to a cause and think 'I would love to change the world like that'. As you scroll down you come across someone else who is famous with a big house and garage full of Ferraris and conclude `that must be what winning at life looks like'. You get up out of bed, put your clothes on, grab a piece of toast and wonder 'how can I impact the world?' and 'what could I do to be that famous and successful?' wondering whether the fame and impact those people are having is what living a successful life looks like....

Here is the good news: your fame starts here. Your fans (children and wife) are waiting right outside your bedroom (or toilet) door and what you do next will have a big impact on their lives.

Today, I'm going to tell you what true fame and success looks like in our lives.

In our world, fame is often seen as a persons importance, a measure of their success. Being famous can be perceived that you have made it, are worth aspiring to be like and **are significant**.

But what is fame really? It's being well-known by a whole lot of people who you don't know, who recognise you, point and whisper to their friends and try to take a picture with you. These people are impressed because of the movie you made, the song that you wrote, or the sports trophy you won. They don't know you personally. They just think you are great from a distance.

How much harder would it be to impress these people if they knew you, personally, up close, where they could see everything about you? Perhaps your great song, movie, or sports feat would shrink in their eyes, if you weren't actually that nice to be around day-to-day.

So mabe true fame, true importance is to be highly esteemed by those closest to you....

Who would you rather impress and inspire - strangers or your family?

Your family. They see everything. They are much harder to impress. With your family it's not one large feat of greatness, but many small acts done daily over years. It's how you treat your family. The words you speak about people and to people. It's the self-discipline you have, how you have fun, the way you help others, how you connect with people. It's all the little things that make up the image of how your family views you living your life

Now, someone who could achieve greatness in the daily moments, being viewed over days and years, now they would be a legend. The real deal. To their family, they would be famous and significant in the deepest sense. Famous people come and go, but your family's impression of you will always be there. And you are who they will model their life on.

How you can become famous to your family

Make a plan to have a healthy family with great relationships.
With your wife, write down what a great family looks like and aim for that, like an athlete aims for a medal or a world championship. To have a loving marriage, to be an inspiration, to tell your kids you love them daily, to play together as a family. Write down your family goals and hang them where they can be easily seen.

Study to be a great dad and husband.
Books, books, books. Read or listen on how to be a great dad and husband. Learn about the five love languages. Research the ways to succeed in your present and future life.

Find a role model to learn from.
Find a guy with a loving marriage, whose kids love them and want to be around them, especially as grown-ups. Spend time with this person and learn from them. How do they treat their wife? How do they interact with their kids? Watch and learn.

Use your strengths.
What are your strengths? Bring these into your family. What do you love doing that comes naturally to you? Do you love dancing? Put on music in the kitchen when you are cleaning up, turn a chore into a game. Do you love history? Tell your family stories. Are you great at building? Build a tree hut with the kids. Do you love sport? Play fun games with your family. You will feel great and have fun.

Be ok with making mistakes. You are on a growth journey.
You are human, you make mistakes. Apologise and give your kids context; 'I got it wrong this time kids. This is something I am working hard on'. Forgive yourself and move on. Athletes get knocked down all the time. It's the great ones that get back up and keep trying. Aim to improve just 1% everyday.

Consistently do little things every day.
Do important little things daily: kisses, cuddles, encouragement, self-education, life lessons, playing and spending time together. Greatness in your family happens when you consistently do the little things.

You are your families hero
There are so many popular stories in books and movies of the guy who works hard, fights the battles, gets knocked down and gets back up again to finally triumph. Like the boxer who runs 5 miles every morning when nobody is watching, trains hard at the gym sparring and hitting punching bags month after month, to compete and win the prize, fight, and fame. You might not be the boxer fighting for a title, but you are the dad putting in the love and service every day, fighting for your family.

This is your story and you are the main character. The people of the world may never hear about it, but winning the love and respect of your family, your people, is true fame.

Be the 'Famous in your Family' Dad

2.

Be the 'Has a Dream' Dad

Have a dream, make a plan and take steps
to live a great life.

Dream and plan for a great future.

To create a great future for your family, it is important to establish a dream of what this looks like and plan how to make it happen.

The wall of memories. Time travel with me to your house 20 years into the future. You are standing in the hallway and are looking at your photo wall of all the experiences your family have shared. What images would you like to see? Family trips, great moments of your kids playing sports games, fun family experiences, a happy mum and dad who are more in love than ever? Now imagine standing there, with your wife who puts her arm around your waist, resting her head on your shoulder and both of you, smiling and proud, happily reminiscing. These moments and the quality of your relationships can become a reality by the decisions you make today. Dreaming of what you would like your future to be is how you start.

Start by imagining, hoping and dreaming.

When starting anything, you need a picture of how you want it to end. Whether you are building a house, restoring a car or even just shaving your face. The end goal of what you want determines what you need to do to get there. By dreaming and creating a vision for what you want your family to become and experience, you can then start planning and taking steps to reach these goals.

Being a dad who doesn't have goals, and just hopes that good things will happen in his life will not get the same outcomes. Be intentional.

The father who dreamed, planned, and is now living his dream. As young parents in their twenties, my wife's Dad and Mum, laid out their goals with a 'lets have no regrets' mindset. They planned and focused their energy into building a family that would live, play and work together. Through the proceeding 40 years, they succeeded in living their family dream. Here is an outline of the plan they used to get there:

Stage One - Dream.

Start by dreaming of how you want your family to be

My wife's parents planned to raise confident, well loved and 'equipped for life' children, and also to be friends with their kids when they reached adulthood. So with this goal in mind, my father-in-law purposely involved himself with his six kids in whatever they were interested in: remote control cars, animal day at school, shooting sports, motorbikes, waterskiing, drag racing cars, boating, skiing, sport, dogs and cats.

If a child had an interest, he would aim to be involved - funding, helping and joining in. And 40 years later, these parents achieved the great friendship and ongoing relationship with their kids that they were aiming for. They were living their dream (sadly, my mother in law, Betsy passed away during the writing of this book). Many other families say to me, 'Wow, Ferg, this is a special family who works and plays together. How did they create that?' I'm glad you asked! Here is the answer:

Dreaming, deliberate actions, determination (and conflict resolution).

The dream goal steered their choices. When you have a clear goal you are focused. When a deviation or distraction comes along like having to work late too often or being away from home too much, having a clear goal in place gives you more purpose and strength to make a decision to stay on course and spend the time needed with your family. The grand prize, your agreed family goal, helps you make a decision in the moment to achieve it. When you know what you want your future to be, you can start taking the right steps towards that goal starting now.

Have a think about what your goals. Dream, plan and make them happen.

Questions to help you identify your family dream

Ponder and answer the questions below. It's good to include your spouse in this.

What kind of dad do you want to be? (friendly, firm but fair, a guide, best mate, inspirational, fun)

What activities/experiences do you want to share with your kids? Now, then as teenagers and later as adults?

What words do you want your family to be described as? (loving, giving, adventurous, competitive, close)

What kind of people do you want them to become? In their careers, their character, as parents and friends.

How do you want them to behave and act? (determined, light-hearted, helpful, compassionate)

What do you want your relationship with your wife to look like when the kids move out?

How do you want your relationship with your wife to be described on the way through?

The answers that you provided help sum up the goals you have for your family.

Create a mission statement. Based on your answers to these questions, write a mission statement of what you want your family to be like and the experiences you want to share. After you have written this mission statement, start making plans, and strategise to make these dreams a reality.

Hang your mission statement somewhere in plain view in your house, where everyone can see it. Read it as you walk past and be reminded of it daily as inspiration of what is important to you.

Here's an example of a family mission statement:

We love and value each other

We love doing fun things together weekly

We love helping each other out

We are hard workers

We listen to each other and seek to understand

We are smart and study to use our incredible brains

Dad and Mum love going on dates once a month

People are more important than things

We stick together and help each other out

We are readers and leaders

We love giving Mum and Dad cuddles and kisses

We share great experiences together

We want to: Race BMX together, play in the same basketball team, go to Europe as a teenage family

It can also be helpful to simplify your goal into a simple one-liner:
'To have fun raising confident and loving children while having many great experiences, with Mum and Dad growing more in love.'

Here you can write your family mission statement:

————————————————————————————

————————————————————————————

————————————————————————————

————————————————————————————

————————————————————————————

————————————————————————————

Stage two of how to live your dream - Make a plan.

"If you fail to plan, you plan to fail." - Benjamin Franklin.

A good plan sets you up for future success. Your future self is yelling back through time, "thank you" for putting in place a great plan now which helped create a better future.

Start planning and taking small steps today with your wife about how you can make these dreams a future reality. Set yourself easily achievable daily, weekly, monthly and annual goals. Remember, small things done often will cause greatness to happen over time.

Dwayne 'The Rock' Johnson says: **"Success isn't always about greatness, it's about consistency. Consistent, hard work gains success. Greatness will come."**

An example of Dream, Plan and Action:

> **Dream:** a great relationship with my kids, with open communication as teenagers.
> **Plan and Action:** to have communal meal times together.
>
> **Dream:** to go on a holiday once a year or a big one to Europe in 5 years.
> **Plan and Action:** start saving $30 - $50 a week to finance this.

Here you can Dream and Plan:

When you know where you are going, that focus helps get you there. Be disciplined to follow the plan and be prepared to make sacrifices and hard choices along the way. I know that you can live the dreams you have for your family by dreaming and planning. **Your future self is thanking you.**

I'm really excited about you being the 'Dad with a Dream'.

3.

Be the 'Spends Time' Dad.
Time = love

Time with your kids is the most precious gift
that you can give.

One of the best ways of communicating love is giving your time.

Your undivided attention. This is time together where you are engaged, not distracted, and giving 100% of your focus. A lot of people feel loved when someone they love spends time with them. Especially kids.

In this chapter, I'm going to let you in on six easy, practical keys on how your kids feel loved by spending time together, that the whole family can enjoy!

What do Kids want most? Your Time!

A video study was conducted a couple of years ago where kids were asked: "What is it that they want most?" Surely the answers would be: A huge pile of Lego, a pony or to go to Disneyland. The overwhelming response was surprising and took away the breath of their parents watching: more time with Mum and Dad!

When you spend time with your kids, they are getting the most precious gift you can give. More valuable than money, holidays, toys or TV. They are getting YOU. You are their role model. The person they most look up to and from whom they feel the most loved and treasured. You help them see how they fit into the world and how to handle possibilities and problems. What you think about them is how they will learn to think about themselves. And how do they learn all of these things? Through time spent together, watching you, interacting and hearing your encouragement. To your kids, your words are as full of power and authority as a king bestowing a title on a knight as he taps the sword on each shoulder; 'I knight you Sir Good At That' or 'Sir Funny Guy'. This is the weight your words carry when you say to your children, '*Wow you are really good at that,*' or '*You are funny*'. And it's by spending time together that we can observe, notice and comment.

One problem though, I don't have any time... That may be what it feels like, but we all have 24 hours in a day. It comes down to what we choose to spend our time on. Time is our most valuable resource, and our kids and spouse are our most valuable investments.

Quality time doesn't necessarily mean a long time. But it does mean quality time where you are engaged and not distracted. Put your phone away, not in your pocket, find a home for it on a shelf! Then go and seek them out. Watch their faces light up, their hearts grow with importance and their personalities come alive as they realise, 'Right now, I am the most important thing in my superhero Dad's life.' With my three year old, a small moment of play is better than none at all. I can have a fun 1 minute hot wheels car race when he invites me in on the way past his room.

Set yourself an achievable daily goal. Start small with 5-10 minutes and let it grow from there. A little time everyday is better than big random chunks rarely.

A fun way to spend time with kids 2-10+ can be getting a spray bottle and brush and doing each other's hair.

So, here are eight great ways to spend quality time together:

Playing together (there is a boy in that man body of yours)

1. **Imaginative play** - Walk into the room and ask, '*what is this strange planet?!*' There will be a moment of, '*what's gone wrong with Dad?*' and then the kids will jump into the imaginary martian landscape. Kids love leading the play. Let them come up with the ideas and then see how you can join in. Get your imagination involved. If you feel like you lack imagination, defer to Pirate, Spaceman, Policeman or Robber. Saying, "*argh me hearties,*' with a bent finger hook and walking with the limp is enough to transform your kitchen into the Jolly Roger Pirate ship.

2. **The sleeping game -** I play a game when tucking the kids in called the sleeping game. I pretend to be asleep on their bed, they give me a kiss on the forehead and I wake up as if I have been teleported to a new world. I look around, bewildered and ask '*where am I?*' The kids then choose what new place I have landed in and we play that out; house town, lolly town and many more. The three year old loves to land me in 'poo town'.

3. **Sports and outdoors activities -** What is their favourite sport or physical activity? At home, grab a ball/bat, or improvise with a dirty sock or undies and have a game of hallway rugby. With sports, have a go, you don't need to be good or bad, just join in. With organised sporting events, kids just love you, their parent, being there watching (shout out to my mum who would be one of three adults watching Friday night 13-year-old basketball and yelling '*go Fergus!!*' from the stands).

4. **Reading books -** Grab a book that they love or that you love, snuggle up with them and get into the story. Have fun with the voices, switch the characters names for those of your kids and ask them questions like 'what would you have done in that moment when the outhouse caught on fire??'

5. **Creating lively conversation and then listening -** You: '*Hey, what was the favourite thing that happened to you today? Or what was the worst thing that happened? If you could go anywhere where would it be and why? If you could be anyone, who would it be?*' Their answers will give you a lot of laughs and huge insight into their lives.

6. **Helping them -** Homework, tidying the room together or a school project they are working on. You will have some of the greatest conversations with your kids just doing the dishes together! There can be a challenge in knowing how much help to give before it's just you doing it or taking over their school project. A good way to think of how much to help, is like spotting someone lifting weights: a small amount of assistance in the right direction can help get great results. The goal is connection and feeling like a team.

7. **Having breakfast and/or tea with them -** Sit down and eat together. At mealtimes all of the family is together in one place at the same time, and it's a good opportunity to give family members the spotlight to talk and ask questions.

8. **Tucking them into bed at night -** Give them a cuddle and a kiss, tell them how much you love them and what you believe about them: '*You are a great leader*', '*You have an excellent imagination*', '*Mum and I love you very much*'. I love to finish off with a goodnight prayer.

There are many other great ways to spend time together: working in the garden, doing jobs around the house or heading into nature. Success is finding something you both enjoy!

Go for it guys, choose to invest your most precious asset - time, in the best investment you have, your family.

Be the 'time spent' Dad.

<u>Note</u>: See 'I Love Mum', Chapter 13, for more about the quality time love languages. There is an amazing book titled 'The Five Languages of Love' by Gary Chapman which shows you best how to show love to your family.

4.

Be the 'Life-Giving Words' Dad – encourage your family

Powerful life-giving words spoken to
your kids and wife create an amazing future of
self-belief and acceptance.

Words are powerful.

Your words are amazingly powerful. When you speak powerful words of encouragement and love to your family (and to yourself), you will have a positive, confident and happy household.

King Solomon was known for his wisdom and he wrote, *"Life and death is in the power of your words, and those that love using their words will see the power and benefit of them."*

'You can do it' - 'I believe in you' - 'You are precious'

These powerful statements spoken into the hearts of your family will create an internal playlist of love and self-belief that keeps playing, even when you are not present. These loving words will become embedded in your family's hearts and minds and they will hear these messages repeating over and over internally. They become words that will encourage them forever.

Try reading this out loud now to experience the power of encouraging words:

'I am a great dad. I have many great skills. I am one of a kind. I have an incredible mind. I have an incredible future and can do whatever I put my mind to.'

How do you feel now? Hopefully empowered and emboldened. Try saying it a couple more times. Words have power.

So how do you harness your words to become creative and powerful?

Firstly, realise that your words are powerful.
Secondly, think of the messages that you want to speak, the future results you want to have.
Thirdly, put these words into action.

The following two stories are examples of the influence and power of positive and negative words said by a dad to his kids.

The Negative Dad who got what he said

About five years ago, a dad came into the retail store where I work, with his wife and two young daughters of four and six. He was a fairly unhappy guy, and when the mother asked the girls to come over, the dad said *'Yeah come on you little sh*ts'*. The girls came over, heads down, looking terribly unhappy. I felt so sad for the future of these girls. What this dad thought about them was forming what they believed about themselves. And what he thought about himself was reflected in the words that came out of his mouth. I have never seen a more unhappy family, and he was getting the result of what he was saying.

Life is in our words.

The boy who loved learning words and receiving positive encouragement

My son had just started school and was learning his early words, a list of about 15 words that help you to start reading. I had learnt with my daughters that you need to make it fun, or it can turn negative for them very fast. So I decided to be completely over the top with my praise when he got one right. "*WOW!*" I would say in a loud voice and sit back with big eyes, "*You know the word 'am'?!*". He would look at me like he had just discovered gold and then would quickly turn back to trying the next one. "*WOW!*" I would say again for the next one and so on down the list.

A couple of nights later, he came up to me in his pre-bed playtime with his first words list in hand and said, "*Dad, can we do my list?*". We had already finished the list earlier and he now had time to go and play but, this was not about learning words, this was about receiving positive encouragement from his dad.

Your voice will become what they believe about themselves in their hearts. If you speak and repeat these positive messages many times, they will start echoing around their minds and hearts. When a situation comes up where they feel like giving up, or are being bullied or put down, the positive encouragement that you have given them day after day will come to the front of their minds: 'You are special.' 'We love you.' 'You can do it'. This will help them to reject these new negative thoughts or words and decide 'No, I am special.' 'I can do it'. Your words will become their thoughts and words.

If we want positive words to come out of our mouths, we need to get our minds thinking positively. Whatever we think inside is what we speak outside.

Here's two great ways to generate positive thoughts:

'This is what I love about them'.
Create a list of each member of your family and of the things that you love and appreciate about them, i.e. 'You have such a great imagination', 'You try hard', etc.

"It's not about what it is, it's about what it can become." - Dr Seuss

'This is what I want and will encourage them to be even if they are not there yet'.
If you want your child to be a good listener, say, '*You are an incredible listener.*' You may be thinking, '*But they are not an incredible listener.*' This may be true now, but I have found that it does not take long before speaking positive words like 'you are a great listener,' that children soon start acting like a great listener.

It's easy to look at someone and call them what they are in that moment, annoying, naughty or frustrating. But saying this is just reinforcing the behaviour with belief and will further ingrain the habit or attribute.

Anyone can state the obvious and be negative, but that will just give you more of what you are already getting. You need to arm yourself with the skills to be positive and change the future lives of your family.

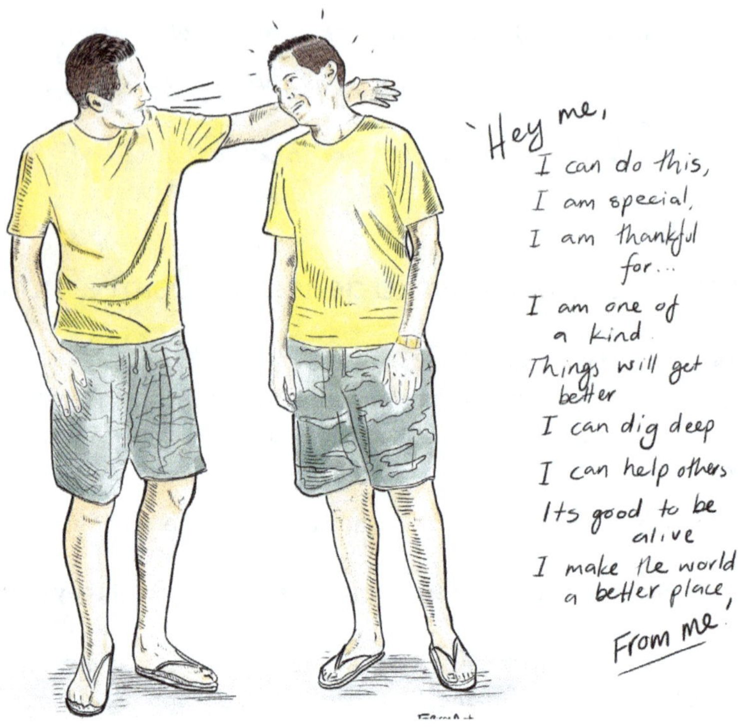

Encourage yourself.

Practical tips to think and speak powerfully and positively:

Start with yourself. What do you believe about yourself? Start thinking and speaking positive words into your own life, and shut off speaking negative, self-degrading words.

Think and write down all the things that you love and are great about your kids and partner.

Think and write down the things that you are thankful for about your kids.

Write down all the traits that you want them to have.

Discipline yourself to speak these life-giving words into your family once a day. When I am tucking my kids into bed at night, I love to say: 'You are really precious.' 'You have a great imagination.' 'You have a great mind.'

Whenever a good thought pops into your head about someone, tell them on the spot.

Here is a list of encouragement that you can speak to your family:

"You..   ..are a special part of our family"

..can do whatever you put your mind to"

..have an incredible mind"

..have a great imagination"

..are special"

..are one of a kind"

..have an amazing future"

..are precious to us"

..give the best cuddles"

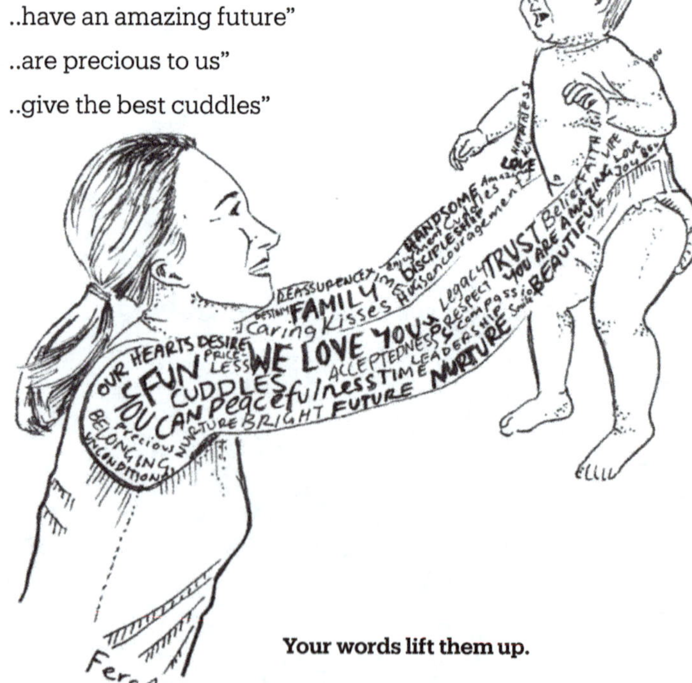

Your words lift them up.

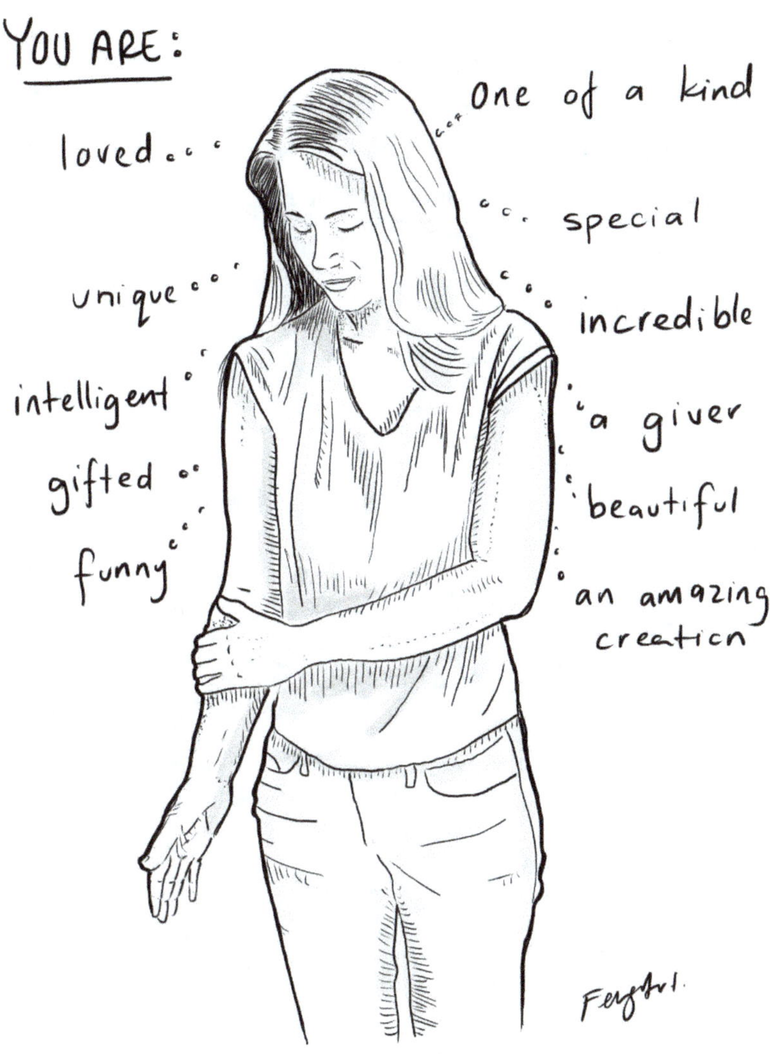

Your words spoken to your children is what they will think about themselves

Here is what you can say to encourage your kids' future behaviour:

"You..   ..make this family a great family"

..are such a great listener"

..are a great help to us"

..can do whatever you put your mind to"

..are great at tidying up"

..are a great friend maker"

..are really kind"

..are a great giver"

..are a great worker"

..never give up"

If you want great results, speak great things.
Be the 'Powerful Life-Giving Words' Dad.

5.

Be the
'Tell Them You Love Them' Dad

'I love you.' Three of the most powerful words
you can tell your family.

Tell them you love them.

'I love you' is a simple and powerful message that changed both my mum's and my own life. I'm going to tell you our story of how we overcame the awkwardness of saying those three words. Plus find out the amazing effect saying 'I love you' will have in your family's lives.

'I love you'. These are three of the most powerful words that you can speak to your family that will affect their lives. When your family hears you speaking these words of love, they are also hearing:

> I am important to Dad
>
> I am accepted for who I am
>
> I am worth spending time with
>
> I am loved
>
> I am precious
>
> I am valued

'I love you' from Dad and Mum sets the gold standard of what love looks like. Saying 'I love you' and then living a parenting and relational life of giving, loving, resolving conflict, healthy intimacy and believing the best, shows your family what true love looks like.

This will contrast against any unhealthy, selfish picture of love your kids will come up against from movies, music, future friends and girlfriends or boyfriends. Your love will show them what love is healthy and also what selfish love looks like, to stay away from.

'Mum and I love you.'

Part 1. The little girl who needed to hear the words.
My mum grew up in a family in Wanaka, in the central South Island of New Zealand, where her Mum and Dad had lived through a war, the great depression of the 30's and had parents who had lived through the first World War. They were hard workers, (my grandfather drove his tractor from Invercargill to Wanaka, over 300km on dirt roads to start a new life) and were good providers.

However, their family heritage and the time period that they lived in lacked an important level of intimacy. My grandfather had never really given my mum much physical affection or told her 'I love you'. 'I love you' coupled with a good hug was what she really wanted to hear and experience. This created a void in my mum's heart that still existed as an adult and when she became a parent herself.

Part 2. My difficult first time saying 'I love you'
My wife and I were dating at the time and her family were excellent at expressing their love for each other. They would often be heard saying; 'Hey, I love you', 'Have a great day, I love you'. These were genuine expressions of love, often made with eye contact and a smile or hug. This was unusual but inspiring to me.

I had the secret gnawing fear that one day I would die and would never have told my family 'I love you'. One evening on the five-hour car journey to my hometown, after practising these words by myself (role playing definitely helps), I summoned the courage when I arrived home at 11pm and walked straight to my parents' bedroom. I stood there at the doorway and told my parents who were half asleep that 'I loved them'. It was like speaking rocks, heavy emotional lifting, so hard! There was silence and then they both told me 'and we love you too'. What a feeling! I knew we had had a huge breakthrough. I then started on my brothers and sisters and a chain reaction started. From that day to now, my family expresses, 'I love you'. We wouldn't ever want to stop it because we have discovered the value to the hearer and the giver, and I know that we are better for it! For my Mum, I coupled it with hugs. Some people can't finish a hug soon enough, but she would just stand there at kitchen bench, receiving the love for as long as I would give it. Your words and hugs can have this amazing effect in your family too.

A little role-playing on a five hour road trip helped prepare me to share words of love more easily.

Hearing 'I love you' from your dad will set anxious hearts at ease.

Speaking 'I love you' will establish a strong foundation for a healthy positive self image and fears of being not worthy or valued will diminish. People who don't receive the love that they want and need from their fathers, can become adults who are continually searching for ways to fill this gap.

One of our jobs as a dad is to lovingly affirm our families, which gives them confidence and courage to tackle their lives.

'Find a man who will treat you even better than I do.'

Is the relationship advice on how to find a good man, from a friend of mine to his daughter (whom he treats very well).

As a father you are setting the standard for how your children should be treated and how they treat those whom they will love. If you have a daughter looking for a future husband, she will be measuring all the keen young men against how you treated her and made her feel. That is her measure of a man. For your sons, they will have an excellent example to follow of a man who can speak and show affection and feeling.

Does repetition diminish 'I love you'? Not if you mean it every time. You may think that repetition doesn't make it mean as much. If you want it to be more meaningful, then add eye contact, touch them on the shoulder, and say it sincerely.

Real words are followed up with real actions. Say 'I love you' and then back it up with quality time, affection and interaction.

So dads, be the 'I Love You' Dad, it will change your marriage and your family and create layers of security and comfort around them. These are only three words, but these loving words will be a rock in your families lives.

6.

Be the 'Positive Touch' Dad

Help your family to feel safe, accepted and loved
through the power of positive touch.

Your hugs are important.

Are you a hugger, a kisser or a backscratcher? You can be the dad that helps your family feel safe, secure, accepted and loved through the power of your positive touch.

Positive Touch = love, acceptance and security.

When you hug your kids and your wife, you are communicating in one of the most powerful ways - by physical connection. In that moment, they have all of your attention and one of the most special things that you can give - affection. You are affirming their value by your desire to be near them. You don't hug people who you don't like or don't know. You hug people you really love, and your family knows this.

If you have had negative or an absence of positive touch experiences in your past, I would love to help you to move forward into being able to show love through touch.

Touch = physical attention and affection

My Dad - The shameless kisser. He is not loud or outspoken but 100% reliably consistent. You could keep time by my dad's morning routine of skipping (which was part of his fitness regime), prayer and porridge. Every morning before we left for school he would come up to each of us kids and give us a kiss on the forehead. This happened every school morning of my life from the age of five all the way through to 17. When I left school I still lived at home, and occasionally I would drop dad off at school (he was a high school teacher), on my way to work. The first time I did this, we were in the crowded dropoff zone, with kids and teachers all around and dad was about to get out when, wait, he had forgotten something, he leaned across and kissed me on the forehead. For an instant I felt embarrassed, a young man sitting in his turbo Subaru being kissed on the forehead in front of all these people! But then I realised, Dad has done this every day of my life, why would he stop and why would he care who he did it in front of? The most important thing to him was for his kids to feel loved.

My school teacher Dad would give us a kiss on the forehead even as adults, despite onlookers when I would drop him off at school.

Positive touch vs. popular culture

Touch has a bad reputation in the media. In the news it is associated with wrong touching and abuse. In movies, it's physical attention of a sexual nature or tough guys giving a brief bear hug with back slaps. What have you seen on TV, social media or the movies recently where positive, safe physical attention has been role-modelled? You would need to look hard to find it.

If we don't teach our kids what positive touch looks like, they will go looking for love through touch in the way that popular mainstream media portrays, which is often sexual affection.

Touch - the incredible healer. Touch is an amazing healer. It can help people move on from past hurts by conveying love and acceptance. My mum had not been hugged much as a kid due to her father being a staunch Kiwi southern man. She was great at showing us affection, but there was a need in her heart to feel loved and accepted through touch. In my teens, I noticed how much Mum loved and responded to a good hug, so I started hugging her more and more. You could almost see the joy and feelings of love rising up within her. I believe that this has helped in filling the void that she felt. Imagine what your positive touch is doing now in your child's life to set them up for a healthy adult life.

Your positive touch sets the standard. The positive physical affection that you give will demonstrate what touch should look like - giving and caring, not taking. It should always benefit the person receiving the affection. Positive touch will help generate a feeling of safety, security and belonging.

Moving on from your past into a future of positive touch

Are you unsure of how to show physical affection appropriately and positively? Growing up you may not have been shown positive examples of physical affection; let's look at some great ways to help you move forward:

Re-writing the belief that being staunch, macho or tough is how you teach your kids the world is a hard unforgiving place (listen to 'A Boy Named Sue' by Johnny cash)

The world can be a hard place out there, but here, in your family with loving trusted members, it is a safe, secure place. Being loved intensely in the family home prepares your kids to weather the hardness out there while knowing they are loved and accepted. Plus, the love that your children know and experience at home will be a light that shines through them into the wider world.

Healing abuse in your past and how my friend Matt can help. Past abuse is tough and painful, and I can't imagine what a hard road this would be. This is touch in the wrong ways and you will need help to repair this damage. This is damage that can be repaired. My friend, Matt Brown has an amazing story of this damage being repaired in his life. You can read his story in his book 'She is not your Rehab'. He has experienced healing in his life and can love his kids healthily.

As well as reading Matt's book, I encourage you to seek professional help to heal past hurts and move past them.

> *Be encouraged that harmful touch in your past doesn't have to stop you from giving positive touch in your future.*

Make a change - When your family's culture was not to show physical affection. Who was it in your family history that established not showing positive touch as a family trait? You could be the one to reverse that trend and role model positive touch that your children pass onto their children. Stop and think, 'Would my family be better or worse for hugging more and showing that we love each other through touch?' Once you have made the decision that you want positive touch in your family's future, begin with small acts of positive touch, start hugging once a day and grow from there. Find a dad who role models good physical affection; a dad who is loving his family through touch, and observe how he does it. You can be the important point in time that your family culture changes.

10 great ways to show positive physical affection:

Touch has been identified as one of the top five ways that people feel loved. Here are a few ways to show love through touch:

1. Cuddles when your family wake up, leave home for the day or go to bed at night
2. Watching TV and reading while sitting next to each other, a great opportunity for back tickles
3. Holding hands or arms around the shoulders when you are walking
4. Piggy back or shoulder rides
5. Kiss on cheek or forehead when putting to bed or leaving for the day
6. Tickles at any time except just before they need to go to sleep which happens to be the most tempting time
7. Wrestling (we like to call them cuddle rumbles so that the aim is not to hurt someone)
8. High fives, secret handshakes and fist bumps
9. Foot and back rubs while putting kids to bed or watching TV
10. The drawing guessing game on their back: draw a number and they guess what it is

How much is too much? How often should you initiate positive touch? Just go for it, hug them in the morning when you first see them and at night when they go to bed. Give them a kiss on the forehead or cheek before you leave for work and when you get home. Aim to be accused by your kids of hugging too much.

Dads, I know that your positive touch is going to be amazing for letting your family know how much you love them. So slap a high five, give the kids a hug and Mum a kiss and be the 'Positive Touch' Dad!

7.

Be the 'Discipline is Discipleship' Dad

Discipleship is wins and lessons
Disciplining your kids means discipleship.

Everybody is learning.

Let's put the 'L' learner plates on our kids and help them develop character, self-discipline and confidence to tackle this world.

Discipline is discipleship.

Did you know the root words of discipline and disciple are the same? This word in Latin is: Discipulus, which means '*learner*'. The latin word Disciplina means '*instruction*' or '*knowledge*'.

The goals of discipline and discipleship are the same: personal growth. We want to disciple our kids by training them how to live and discipline them through showing their actions can have good and bad consequences. First we will look at discipleship and discipline and then, to help out with their personal growth, I've got some practical tools to assist you: a guide to training the right behaviour, great keys to change and train good behaviour and ways to administer consequences well.

Discipleship and Training

You are the Sensei, their trainer. Discipleship is you, the parent, instructing and the kids learning. If your life was a Kung fu movie (which would be pretty cool) your house would be the dojo (place of training), you are the sensei (teacher) and your kids are the grasshoppers (students). So let's take off our shoes and crash dive through some paper walls! What teacher/ student examples can you think of that you can relate to? Jesus and the 12 disciples, Obi-wan and Luke from Star Wars (or Anakin - ok, not a good example), Morpheus and Neo from The Matrix or Gandalf and the Hobbits from The Lord of the Rings.

These stories help us to picture discipleship and discipline. The goal of the master is always to help grow the student, direct them to the right course, to equip them for the coming challenges and to grow to maturity where they do not need a master. Discipline when only seen as inflicting punishment for wrong, falls short of this larger picture.

What is the goal of discipleship? The goal is to raise a child who is self-governing and has self-control. This is teaching your kids to know what the right thing is to do at the right time. It's about guiding and giving your kids a plan of action that will produce the best result for them and for those around them. It's training your child, who even though they are tempted to make a poor choice, will choose the best course of action and have the inner strength to carry this through.

behaviour *noun*

1. *the way in which one acts or conducts oneself, especially towards others.*

OXFORD LANGUAGES

Realise that training takes time. Training takes months and years. Ouch. Training is not a one-off event. It is speaking, repeating and affirming the same value or action over and over until you have established a new pattern of behaviour. This could be two days if you are lucky, but more likely two weeks to two months until you see a change. There are some behaviours that we have been working on in our family for 1 - 2 years. But know this, it's totally worth it. The hard yards you put into training, will have you experiencing better behaviour for the rest of your years. Discipleship is about consistent guidance over time. Your child has got 16-18 years learning under your instruction. It's important to give them and yourself grace over this time. Let's not forget, we as parents are learning with our 'L' plates on as well, how to lead and teach (and behave).

Discipline and Consequences

Discipline is about learning through consequences rather than punishment. In our family, my wife and I talk about discipline by focusing on 'consequences' rather than 'punishment'. It took me time to break the habit of focusing on 'punishment' but the conscious use of thinking about 'what consequence should we use?' makes a big difference to how you approach discipline. Here is the difference between punishment and consequence:

Punishment can be payback to help you feel better, consequences teach your child to act better.

Punishment is about this time, consequences are about next time.

It is easy to think of discipline as punishment, and although punishment can be a means to correct disobedience, the word discipline loses its power and meaning if reduced to this.

Punishment for wrong doing can be our angry response to a child's disappointing action. We feel upset and we want them to pay for their wrong doing. It can be a temporary fix to help us feel better about the pain they have caused us, themselves or others.

We don't want to punish our kids. We want to train them through understanding their actions have consequences.

Consequences for good or bad behaviour are focused on learning through their actions. Having good pre-meditated outcomes (consequences) for success or failure, helps you to keep cool and focused on their growth. Rewarding good behaviour with good consequences helps to establish good behaviour, "What is rewarded is repeated" - John Jones. Consequences for failure shouldn't be viewed negatively. Failure can be a great educator. 'You just figured out a great way not to do something!' Both parents and kids fail often, and we want to use those failures as precious opportunities to learn and succeed. Good discipline is carefully planned consequences.

Different kids, different methods.

Be prepared to be flexible in your approach to training your children. Our oldest was highly motivated by lollies as an incentive to carry out a task. The next child, number two, couldn't have cared less about lollies as a motivating factor, but valued TV time. For the same children, one would change behaviour after a quick chat about how to better handle a toy sharing situation, whereas the other needed a 10 minute in depth conversation about the emotional causes and effects of who got to play with Barbie. When training your kids, be intuitive about what works best for them.

Deep conversations reliving barbie battles can help prepare for next time

A three step guide to training the right behaviour:

1. Establish Standards
2. Create a Training Plan
3. Prepare Rewards/Consequences

1.   What are your standards?
<u>Decide on your standards ahead of time</u> as when they get tested, you are going to need to believe they are worth the training and retraining to achieve. Firstly, get on the same page as your wife. Make sure that your expectations are realistic and achievable for the age and stage of life your kids are at. You can discover these by reading age-group specific parenting books, or talking to friends whose parenting you admire who have already raised children through this age bracket.

<u>Here's some talking points to think about when establishing standards:</u>
Manners, listening, obeying the first time, not screaming in public.
How to treat others - sharing, kind words, clean language, helping out and
not hitting.

2. What is the plan to train the right behaviour?

This is where you want to be really smart. The best sporting teams don't
just turn up on game day and hope that they will win the game. They have
a training plan and a game plan, training the right things in advance will
best prepare you to get a winning result. This is exactly the same with
parenting. You want to think ahead to the behavioural and character
standards that you want your kids to achieve and then plan the journey of
training them.

Formulate your plan by thinking of past events and how you would
improve on these, picturing future scenarios and how you would deal with
them, and learning from others.

Learning from others is an amazing way to start as you get a wide variety
of methods and outcomes. The more parents you listen to through books,
blogs, podcasts or videos, the more prepared you will be!

Here's an example of a plan to establish behaviour:

<u>Training kindness: The 'Kindness of the Day Award'</u>
We were having some issues with our older three kids acting selfishly.
Things like: being the first to get something, wanting the biggest piece
of everything, basically a lot of 'me' mindedness. So we decided to have
an award at the end of the day where each kid would be able to tell us
what kind action they did. We would write it up on a whiteboard and then
I would judge the kindness act of that day. There would often be many
winners with a piece of chocolate as the prize.

To further help reinforce this, we started saying very frequently, "treat
others the way that you want to be treated". If we found a conflict going on
we would prompt the kids with, "treat others… and they would finish off for
us with "…the way you want to be treated".

The Why

Add the 'Why' into your plan and training. Tell your kids what you are doing and why you are doing it. 'Hey kids, we are going to work on treating people kinder by having a kindness of the day award because this will make each other's days happier' or 'if you treat them better, they will treat you better.' This works even for a 6 month old trying to touch a power plug: 'no touch, sore!'.

3.   What are the Rewards or Consequences?

After doing the first two: 1) Standards and 2) Training, you are going to find you have arrived at one of two destinations: **reward or consequence.** Either the child is learning and 'getting it' or the plan needs repeating or adjusting. The goal with both of these consequences is to reinforce good behaviour and establish self-control. Make sure you plan ahead of time what the outcomes will be. I recommend making a list of both.

Rewards for good behaviour When your child has done the right thing, make a really big deal of it. Give them a hug, a high five, a pat on the back and then give them affirming words with eye contact. Get down to their level if you need to and use words like: 'you did so well', 'thanks so much for listening', 'you are really good at this', 'well done, I'm so proud of you'. Rewards can also be: a tick on the tick chart, food, or device time.

Consequences for falling short Oh no, it didn't work out. This is where you need to have a predetermined plan of action. Don't use consequences that will leave you trapped or that you can't follow through on. Knowing the consequences before the situation comes up avoids these traps. Consequences could be: missing out on TV time, an in depth talk about what happened, running around the outside of the house or doing a chore they don't usually do.

A brief run in the fresh air can be a great attitude reset

Here's an example of administering consequences:

'I asked you to tidy up and because you didn't':

Unplanned, unprepared approach (I often have made this mistake):

a. On the spot consequence: 'You need to go to bed one hour early.' Now you, the parent, have to stop your normal family dinner routine and put the kid (who is not at all tired) to bed for the night (and quite possibly have them wake up early - a double disadvantage to you).

Planned approach:

b. Predetermined consequence: 'You were going to be able to watch TV or read a book before bed but you have used up all your time, so now you will miss out, or spend that TV time tidying up.' See further on in this chapter for a rewards and consequences chart.

Eight keys to change and train good behaviour

1. **Agreeing on one set of standards**

   When Mum and Dad's standards are the same, you are in a powerful position to effect behaviour changes in the family. Sit down with Mum and agree what your standards will be. When you are in agreement you have twice as many people reinforcing behaviour. When you are out of agreement it is very confusing for the kids and it also creates a good cop/bad cop scenario. Imagine living in a country and having two different sets of road rules to obey. It would cause anarchy. Don't set a standard until you can both agree. This is a great motto for family training: 'Who is in charge, what are the rules, will they be enforced?'

**Two different sets of rules would cause havoc
on roads, its also true in the home**

2. **Consistency**

   If you have set a standard, you need to follow it up. The standard gets enforced all the time. If you have told the kids to not jump on the couch, don't turn a blind eye when you are tired. If you can't commit the time or energy to maintain a standard, it's better not to have that standard.

3. **Getting the kids to do it the first time - the key here is to follow through.**

   How many times do you want to ask your child to do something? Do you want them to respond the first time, third time or the 'when you get angry and raise your voice' time?

   <u>Here is the process:</u>

   1. Make a clear request with eye contact: 'Jack (two, five or 10 years old), I need you to come here now.' Jack doesn't come (He's gaming, a two year old genius).
   2. Follow through: Walk over, get on their level, 'Hey Jack, when I ask you to come here, I need you to do that straight away.'

   Life hacks for getting kids to do it on the first ask: make reasonable requests, give advance warning, 'tea is in a minute'.

Close requests down at their level instead of yelling across the room can be more effective

4. **Give the child options - 'run or hop to bed?'.**

   Offering options puts some power in their hands. You have chosen the outcome, they get to choose how to make that happen. 'Hey Buddy, do you want to come and do the dishes now, or in a minute?' This makes it about when they will do the dishes, not if they will do the dishes. You can even make it a fun choice - 'Do you want to run to bed or hop to bed?' They may say neither and that's where consequences for not coming can come in.

5. **Getting their brain activated in choosing good behaviour.**
    If you do all the thinking for the kids, then they will only be great at following orders. What you want is for your children to be able to assess a situation and make a wise decision.

    Ask them to think of the outcomes - 'Hey, if you do that to your sister, what good thing could happen or what bad thing could happen?' 'If you don't do this, what good thing/bad thing could happen?' 'So what do you think you should do?' Give them a moment to consider and then talk over the options they come up with.

Thinking of possible outcomes is great training for future decision making

6. **Affirming who they are and can be**
    Speak out how you want your child to be: 'Hey Gemma, you are an amazing tidier. You are excellent at looking after your siblings. You are a great listener. You are really wise.'

    Your words spoken into their lives help to create their self image.

    If they counter this with 'No I'm not a good tidier,' go back with, 'you are getting better every day,' or, 'I think that you will be.'

7. **Write up the goals**

    If everyone knows the goals, it's much easier to aim for them. We would write up a visual task chart for all of the things that needed to be done before school. Then instead of following up on the individual tasks, we would ask, 'What's next on the list?' This is much easier and trains the kids to think for themselves. You can say, 'If you get everything done by 8am, you can watch 10 mins of.. or go outside and play.'

8. **Reward charts**

    A sticker chart or jar that you put a button in each time when someone takes a positive action, is a great way to train behaviour. When the jar or chart is full, think of a great reward you can give them. A hot drink date with Mum, a special movie, etc. Don't rule out your teens for this, even adults like rewards and affirmation; I would totally love a button jar to fill.

Nine ways to administer consequences well

1. **Get the full picture, and don't jump to conclusions**

    There are two sides to every story. If there are two children involved, make sure that you get both sides of the story before making a judgement. Situations are not always what they seem. I recently asked three five-year-olds for their story about an incident that I had observed happen. They each had a different version of the truth, and none of them were accurate!

2. **Wins and lessons: failure is an opportunity to learn**

    When the child misses the mark and fails, don't be discouraged; growing is wins and lessons. Our children's growth is a journey of development. Failing is like a moment of revelation when a golden light shines on an action or character trait that you can now see clearly, and are able to help steer towards a positive outcome.

3. **Be soft and strong**

    When you are administering consequences to your kids, firstly think of how much you love them, what their potential is and what you are training them for. This will take the edge off any strong emotions you may have (if emotions are high, see Allowing yourself time, below). Be strong in sticking to the outcome that you have decided, and follow through, knowing that they will be better off for the lesson. Give them a hug at the end and tell them how much you love them.

4.   **The power of a long in depth talk**
Sitting down with your child and having a conversation that gets into the nitty gritty of the issue can be a powerful consequence for your child, and more effective than taking away a benefit. This can be uncomfortable for the child as you are digging into the 'why', and they may not have had these thoughts before. This could take 10-20 minutes as you get to the heart of the issue.

5.   **Allowing yourself time**
When the kids have let you down, you don't always have to do something on the spot. You might be tired and angry and are more likely to respond poorly and make a bad decision. You can go away and have a think about how to handle the incident, and have a cooling down period. If the child needs to be separated from the situation, you can send them to their bedroom for a time, and then deal with them once you have calmed down.

**When something displeasing happens,
take a moment, don't let your angry bear out**

6. **Consequences planned in advance**

   These are great to have up your sleeve for when you are in the heat of the moment.

   Time out, no dessert, bed early, device taken away, no TV tonight, points taken off the tick chart.

REWARDS	CONSEQUENCES
Device time	No device time
A lolly or snack	Running around the outside of the house
A tick on the reward chart	A chore (not their usual chore)
Stay up a little later	A serious talk about what happened
High five and encouragement	Earlier bedtime

7. **Removing benefits**

   To continue from above, being a member of the family who contributes to the happiness and helpfulness of your home comes with benefits. Such as: TV, iPad, dessert, later bedtime, playtime, device time. If the kids misbehave then you can remove their right to one of these benefits. I have heard of an exasperated single Mum removing the right to have hot showers for her teenage girls, as these were benefits of good behaviour in their family home (on the upside, unintentional ice shower method health benefits).

8. **The goal is learning, not pain**

   The purpose of consequences is not revenge because they have really annoyed you. It's an opportunity to help them learn and understand that actions have consequences.

9. **Communicating why this has happened**

   It's very important to ask 'why' questions at the point of consequence. 'Why are you here in time out? Why do you think this happened?' If they can't figure it out, then walk them through what happened this time, and why and what could happen next time: 'What do you think you should do next time? What could you have done differently?

So dads, use training and rewards/consequences to create some mini disciples who are growing and are ready to take on the world.

8.

Be the 'Life Coach' Dad – Being their coach

Leading and guiding your kids daily will bring major growth in their lives and satisfaction in yours.

Encourage, inspire and champion your kids.

Dad Media Release: Congratulations! You, Dad have been selected to be Head Coach of a prestigious team full of potential: your family.

Leading and guiding your kids daily, like a coach would his players, will cause major growth, success and security in their lives. It will also be a major source of satisfaction in your life.

What's the difference between a good coach and a bad coach?

A good coach: spots talent, communicates well, plans for victory, identifies weaknesses and nurtures strengths, while overcoming difficulties and obstacles.

A bad coach: can't see a path to success, criticises, blames, gets overwhelmed by frustration, and is eventually fired.
Except you can't get fired, so you may as well learn
to be a good coach.

Imagine you are a professional sports coach, how would you conduct yourself?

A change of perspective

Coaching is a very satisfying part of your job description as a Dad: to look ahead at the next stage of your children's lives and plan how to prepare them to go through it.

Taking on the mindset of, 'being a healthy developer of your children like a good sports coach' can make the parenting years a lot of fun. Picturing yourself as the coach of a national or professional sports team can spark your imagination, and bring inspiration and creativity into your parenting.

Think of your team. Just like any sports team there is the super star, the developing player, a player who throws tantrums on the field, and the rookie. If you were a professional sports coach how would you coach the real life adult versions of these people? The ideas you come up with could apply to your family team. You might say to the one who throws a tantrum, does something silly and gets a yellow card: '*Hey, direct your energy into doing what you know how to do, don't stress about other people, take a deep breath, calm down and have another go*'. To the superstar, '*Have some fun, don't take yourself too seriously*'.

The greatest coaches end up producing the greatest teams.

They see the end goal, usually a championship, and help everyone personally develop one step at a time to work together to reach their goal. Great coaches lead, and bring out the greatness living on the inside of their players. Coaches empower their teams to play the game, and then cheer them on from the side lines. The greatest coaches are often described by their players as a 'father figure' because they cared for their players so much. What a testament that these best, most beloved coaches are described as dads. That is you! The key to being a great coach of your family is being a caring, leading and developing dad. So give your family team a name - ours is 'Team Turnbull' - and let's look at how to be a great coach.

Here are 13 great keys on how to coach your family team of champions:

1. **Ask your child to think of solutions to their 'on field' problems**
   Before you jump in with solutions to solve a problem, give your kids a go at coming up with a solution. Like players on the field in a sports game, they have got a unique perspective on the problem and have possibly already thought of solutions.

   One of our kids was struggling at school. She had started the year really well, but we had received an email from the teacher saying that she had gone backwards. At the start of the year, we had put in place a vision to be a helpful student who was learning well, but the plan had gone off the rails with the arrival of new friends on the scene. We felt tempted to say, 'Hey, you need to ditch these friends and do this...' but we slowed our pulses, took a breath and asked her what was going on. After she had told us her story we asked questions like: 'Why do you think the teacher would have contacted us?', 'What do you think is slowing down your learning?' and 'How do you think you could get back on track?' She provided some great answers and solutions and we added suggestions in any areas needing our wisdom. Next we rolled out a plan for success, which was daily goals of the four most important things to work on (which she had suggested as part of the questioning), and some device time as a reward if she achieved these things. We sent her off to school with these four keys written on the inside of her hand and she turned the situation around for the better in a week.

   <u>Note</u>: To make long term success certain, we kept the plan in place for much longer.

2. **Debriefing their day to help give perspective**
   I love the saying by Ian Grant of the Parenting Place, "Kids are excellent observers and terrible interpreters". When you have a conversation at the end of the day with your children, you can hear what they have observed and what they think this means (just like a coach watching the 'game tape' with their players after the game). This helps you understand where they are at with their schooling and friends; what

is easy or hard and anything they need help with. Make time to have a daily 'catch up' conversation; tea time or bedtime is good.

Here are some great conversation starters:

- What was your favourite thing about today? Least favourite?
- What was hard? What was easy?
- Funniest moment?
- Or just 'How was your day?'

Just listening helps you understand what is going on in your kids' lives.

3. **Being unified with the Team Manager (Mum)**
   When both parents are unified in purpose and communication, the child is much more likely to grow in a clear direction. It's 100% more effective than divided parents. Make time to have conversations with your spouse about your kids, what they are going through and how you are going to deal with a situation, goal or challenging obstacle. If you can't agree, then it is better to take a pause from taking action until you can. Moving forward when divided causes larger problems later as 'a house divided against itself cannot stand'. To reach agreement with your spouse may need hard work, good effective communication and problem solving, but it is worth the energy you put into it.

4. **Teaching through your stories of Wins and Lessons - 'When I was 10...'**
   Stories are one of the greatest ways to teach. Your experiences are personal and full of emotion, and your kids will love to hear them. Stories are memorable. Your kids will recall these in similar situations, and they will remember the lessons. 'Dad had a hard time when he was a boy with his shaggy haired next-door neighbour, but he got through it by doing...' Think of the moral of your story before you share it to make sure that the lesson you are trying to teach will help them!

5. **Helping them stick to commitments**
   Commitment is an important quality in life. Commitment will help your children keep jobs, have a healthy marriage and make great friends. These are invaluable lessons for adulthood. If our children feel like giving up we tell them, 'Push through to the end of the season or school term,' or, 'Your team is relying on you,' or, 'We need to stick to

what we started.' We are careful to choose which sports and activities that we sign the kids up to so that we can successfully honour the commitment. Always be on the lookout to spot the difference between a change of mind and a genuine reason for ending early.

6. **Create team mantras - 'In our family, we dig deep'**
    I love this area of adding powerful mantras or quotes into our family culture. Like the core values and keys to success written on the walls of a sports team changing room, write up your family team's inspiring motivators around your house.

Powerful and inspiring quotes and sayings prepare you for the day.
(In this case the battle of Stirling Bridge 1297, Scotland).

Empowering one-liners are belief boosters your kids can pull out to inspire confidence when they are faced with a challenge. We love to say to our kids "Turnbulls dig deep." When they are struggling, we say, 'Wow, great job, you are digging deep right now.' This gives them more energy to go further. When they have come out the other side either with a win or loss (lesson), we will congratulate them on digging deep. The kids now encourage each other to dig deep too!

These sayings help guide their lives and will be passed down through generations, so find some great ones to use and encourage.

Here are a few to consider:
- 'Our words have power'
- "Our family always does our best'
- 'Whether you think you can or think you can't, you are right.' (Henry Ford)
- 'The extra mile is not often crowded'
- We also love our faith quotes: 'I can do all things through Christ who gives me strength'

7.   Speak positively to their strengths and character

You can reinforce good behaviour and create 'fame' for your children in your family by giving them positive nicknames and making a big deal of their strengths.

One of our kids we have labelled 'The Finder'. She has a natural ability and tenacity to find lost things, so whenever something is lost, we call for 'The Finder'. This is a huge source of pride for her and also means she will search long and hard because of her established self-belief.

Other names we use are 'The Can-do Girl', 'the Kind Brother', 'The Chef' or 'The One Who Pushes Through'.

You can also look at traits that seem negative, like bossiness for example and reframe to: 'You are going to be a great leader' and add 'kind and encouraging' to help them understand how to lead. I would often boss my younger brother around, which I would be corrected for doing, but it gave my father insight into my personality. My dad would often say to me later (not in the moment of me bossing), 'you are going to be a great leader.' It made me feel amazing and created the belief that I could be a great leader.

Lastly, speak out in faith the positive traits you would like to see in your child which might be completely absent or still developing, 'you are becoming a really helpful part of our team'. If your child finds it hard to tidy up, speak to them of the greatness that they will be, 'you are becoming a great tidier'.

8. **Creating thinkers**

   We want our children to be able to think their way through a challenge when we are not present. Great sports teams like the All Blacks teach and empower the players to make decisions during a game, when the coaching team cannot be there on the field in the 'heat of the moment to give advice.

   You can help teach your kids to be problem-solvers by talking through their latest scenario like this:

   - Firstly, gather as much information as possible, understand their situation by listening.
   - Secondly ask a series of leading, thought-provoking questions to get them to envision future outcomes :
   - What good/bad things could happen if you do this?
   - What good/bad things could happen if you don't do this?
   - What have you tried in the past, how did that work?
   - What do you think the best option is now?
   - Thirdly, go over their answer with them and help by giving direction where needed: 'If you did this action, this outcome could happen; I think that this suggestion (of fatherly wisdom) could help'.

   Teaching your kids to consider how their different actions will cause different outcomes is teaching and empowering them to problem-solve.

9. **Helping your kids succeed in their current position**

   Helping kids to 'win' and succeed creates a great feeling of positivity and confidence for them. Understand what is important for your kids in their current life stage, and help them to achieve those things.

   Our kids are almost all at school. Making the most of every year of their life is really important to my wife and I. We don't want their 12-13 years of school to be a miserable or boring experience that they can't wait to escape from. We want our kids to enjoy and thrive in every area of their lives from age two to 92! So I try to get the kids into a 'success feeling' as early as possible, so that they get a 'winning' feeling and are engaged. Reading is the first thing that new entrants at school tackle so we go over the first words lists with the kids and set goals and rewards for when they have mastered their word levels. They quickly learn how to read, which is amazing for self-development and is an enjoyable quiet pastime.

Spend time thinking about what you can do to help your family engage and succeed in their current life stage.

10. **Their dream vs. your dream**

    I really wanted to be in the NBA (National Basketball Association) in the United States. I got up early and trained in the morning and played at every school break. Despite my genetics, parents who are both shorter than 5'6", I hoped and prayed to be 6'4" like Michael Jordan. Unfortunately I only grew to 5'7" (which was a 1 inch gain from all the praying), but I didn't have a lot of natural ability, so never ended up running out on the court for the Phoenix Suns Team. However, I still absolutely loved playing the game so much.

    I would love my kids to be in the NBA, it would be incredible, but, this was my dream. I need to discover their talents and dreams and do what I can to encourage their growth in these. Kobe Bryant, an NBA superstar, when asked if his kids would play basketball said, "I don't mind what they do as long as they find their passion". When you expose your kids to lots of different experiences, you learn what they might love or be good at. Sometimes, just playing your favourite sport because it's fun, brings the greatest joy, and you can do that anytime.

11. **Spot their skills and nurture them early - Potty Boy**

    Look for what comes naturally to your child and nurture that. You often need to try many different activities and experiences to find out what this is. When I was two or three, my parents identified that I liked drawing, so when I was toilet training on the potty, they would give me a tray, paper and pencils to draw with while I was sitting. They probably secretly hoped to teach me multitasking too! Throughout my childhood my dad would always bring home scrap paper for me to draw on and would encourage me to submit my drawings to be displayed in the local paper. I would take my drawings to my parents and they would 'ooh' and 'ahh' about how great they were, and encourage me to keep going. I'm so glad that they did, as this is a major source of satisfaction for me as an adult.

Also – that thing your kids can be great at, might not become obvious until they are much older. If this is the case and you haven't found anything yet, be encouraging towards their positive personality and character traits and keep exposing them to different experiences.

Mum and Dad early on recognised I liked drawing and would set me up during my 'potty time' with pen and paper (inadvertently teaching me multi-tasking).

12. **Struggles are a great opportunity for learning**
Struggles are a gift. They are positive or negative depending on how you look at them. It can be tough when a hard situation at school arises, but this is a great learning opportunity for your child to develop character and problem-solve how to successfully get through. If you and your child can deal with a struggle now and develop the character and tools to overcome it, then when a bigger problem happens in the future, as a teen or an adult, they are going to be much better equipped to deal with it. Issues of character are dealt with either now or later (now is better).

13. **Different kids, different methods**

    Much like on a sports team each of your children will have different combinations of personality, character and strengths and weaknesses. What comes easily to one child could be very difficult for the next. Some of the systems and incentives that we put in place for our first child, did not inspire or motivate our second child. We had to take a step back and think, what will help motivate this next child and help them grow? Have a think on their personality and what natural strengths they have, and work with these. Or just try many different parenting techniques until you come upon one that works and is empowering for that child.

So Coach, this is your team and your season. Work out what motivates and grows your players and how you can work well with the team manager, and you will have great team success and hopefully, a whole lot of fun.

9.

Be the 'Role Model' Dad

You, the dads, are the real role models who will inspire a generation. Don't leave it to the politicians, movies or music industry.

'Example isn't the main thing in influencing others.
It is the only thing' - Albert Schweitzer.

It's not politicians, movies, media or music who will have the most impact on the next generation, it is us the parents. You (the dads) are the hidden role models who will inspire and change a generation.

When you think of a role model, who do you think of? A sports or movie star? It's true, they are public figures that people listen to, admire and look up to, but I challenge their suitability as our kids' (or our own) role models in areas outside of their expertise. They have influence due to media exposure, but they are role modelling how to attain to and do the specific thing that made them famous, like playing a sport professionally, or acting a role convincingly. While these achievements are worthy of admiration, it doesn't mean that how they behave in the other areas of their life should be looked up to or copied. I recommend watching Charles Barkley's YouTube video on 'I am not a role model'. Charles Barkley, previously an NBA basketball player from the 1990's, created shock in society when he announced publicly that he is not a role model, that he's just a basketball player, and it's not his job to raise your kids.

You are the complete package, demonstrating all areas of life, role model. You and your wife are the most genuine complete pictures of adults that your kids will ever see. Your children see every part of your life; the good and the bad, the kind and the mad. Your life is on show for them to watch everyday. You are the total picture; not a carefully sculpted social media image that a team full of public relations experts create. How you live life every day, is the example your kids will subconsciously imitate, or consciously choose to model their lives after. And your kids are in attendance at your school of life everyday.

You might say, 'I'm not even trying to teach them anything,' but this is what they are learning through your behaviour.

Right now you are role modelling:

- How to treat others
- How others can treat you
- How you treat yourself
- How to work
- How to enjoy life and have fun
- How to respond to authority
- What to do when things go well
- What to do when things go poorly
- What type of physical condition you keep your body in
- How to have a great attitude - or how to have a bad attitude
- What is important and what is not important
- How to keep persevering or to give up
- To play by or bend the rules
- How to love and be loved

How to become the role model to raise great kids

Becoming the role model you wish to be is like choosing a superhero to imitate.

Do you want to be like Captain America (Steve Rodgers), a brave upstanding symbol of justice and freedom, or Tony Stark/Iron Man 'billionaire, philanthropist, playboy' - Avengers Movie quote. Like the ideals and strengths these comic book heros portray, look at the virtues that you want to see replicated in your family, and then develop and demonstrate those things in your life. If you want to take this to the next level, draw a sweet superhero picture of yourself with a key of your desired traits and then sew up a superhero costume to wear around the house (just wearing undies is not a superhero outfit) or try:

A two step journey of how to be a great role model for your kids:

1. **Understand** what you are role modelling now and what you want to role model in future. Or 'who you are and who you want to be'.

2. **Develop** these areas in your life for your family to see a great example of how to live.

What kind of role model are you now? What is the picture you are showing your kids? This is a great opportunity to look at yourself and ask the question: Do I want my kids to imitate me? This is hard, because it's about turning the spotlight on your life.

Seven questions to ask yourself to determine what kind of role model you are:

1. What's the 3 greatest things I do that make me a great role model?

2. What are the 3 behaviours that I hope my kids don't imitate?

3. What are the 3 most important behaviours I want to role model to my kids?

4.   What are 3 things that I would love to be better at as a role model?

5.   What behaviours and habits I have inherited from my parents I would want to change for my children? i.e. fear, anger, worry, poor money management

6.   How do I role model being a good dad? i.e. :spending time, loving mum, being a hard worker

7.   How do I role model being a good man?

Ten keys to developing into a great role model

1. **Role model being an individual**

   Be you. Be authentic. Don't try and be someone else. Major in your strengths, the positives in your life that come naturally. You might love science facts, telling jokes or be soft hearted and have a tendency to cry in movies. Embracing that it is 'ok being unique' is a great example you can show your kids.

Bring your best self to the day.

2. **Role model how to deal with weaknesses**

   What are your blind spots, your work-ons? Take one or two of these and start working on them. It could be patience, leaving things until the last minute, or negative words you use. Be open and honest about these with your kids, 'Dad is struggling with patience, but I am working on it' or, 'I'm sorry that I got angry, that is an area that I'm working on'. Everyone has issues and you are role modelling working through yours.

3. **Treat other people well**

   How do you treat your wife, your kids, your neighbours and people
   that you can get nothing from? Your example will be watched and
   copied by your kids. My father and his father were great at striking up
   conversations with, and taking an interest in strangers. I watched this
   as a child, and now it's something I love to do. Think of the number of
   people your children could positively impact throughout their lives,
   by following your great example of, 'Treat others the way you want to
   be treated'.

4. **Role model grit through difficult opportunities**

   Difficulties and challenges can be an opportunity to role model how
   to dig deep and persevere. When the next hard situation arises, take a
   moment, a couple of deep breaths and think, 'This has happened, what
   do I need to do to make the best of this situation and work towards the
   solution?' Your response and solution could be a story talked about in
   your family for years; 'The tire blew out on the family holiday and dad
   sang his favourite song while he changed the tire!' Your attitude will
   hinge on being problem or solution-orientated, and your kids will be
   watching to see how you react.

5. **Role model trying your best, not being perfect**

   There is no such thing as the perfect human. The stories of the greatest heroes are filled with enduring failure, and getting it wrong on the way to getting it right. It's really important to show kids that failure is part of the journey of learning, so that when they fall short, they don't get discouraged and not try again. Life is full of wins and lessons.

6. **Role model community and establish your family culture**

   Who are your friends? Are they a positive, negative or neutral influence? How do you treat them, and how do they treat you? When I started Nordic ski racing as a 17 year old, it wasn't long before I started wearing very tight full body lycra race suits like all the other ski racers - clothing I would never have dreamt I would wear. We become like who we hang around.

   Create or find a great community that is a healthy, encouraging place for you and your family. A local school, sports club, community group or church is a good place to start. We are part of a great church that treasures and teaches service, encouraging and helping each other and family skills. My friend Hunter has done an incredible job making his local Rugby club into an amazing community that families want to become a part of.

7. **Find an excellent role model for you**

   Find a positive role model whom you can look up to. If you can find a dad you admire, further along in life experience (not necessarily age), try and spend time around this person. If you don't have someone physically present, you can read biographies and autobiographies, which are stories of amazing people to learn lessons from their lives (this is where the sports stars as great role models come in). I was inspired to dig deep from listening to Bear Grylls' 'Blood Sweat and Tears' autobiographical book about qualifying for the SAS.

8. **Do what you say you will**

   Be a man of your word, then your kids will always know that you are reliable and can be trusted. This role models and helps to form integrity in your kids and they will grow to act the same. The best friends, bosses, employees and people are true to their word and able to be trusted.

9. **Put life into perspective as it happens**

    Share with your kids mantras and stories from your past of lessons, wins and losses. Your wisdom, beliefs, values and perspective will help your kids to understand how to think about life. 'If you want a friend, be a friend'. Tell your kids stories from your life: 'I remember when I turned up to school on my first day... My cousin Henry came and sat with me when I was alone...' Your stories will help guide your kids.

10. **Work out what you believe**

    What are your values and your beliefs? What is important and meaningful to you in life? What do you believe about how the world came into being and what happens after we die? Your kids will ask you about these big questions and listen to your answers to form their beliefs. These beliefs influence how we live our lives. My Christian faith steers a large portion of my parenting; how I treat others, how I parent and how I deal with worry, fear or love everyday. I'm so thankful for it and the direction it gives me and that I can pass this on to my children.

So dads, you and Mum are your children's primary life role models.

Figure out how you want to demonstrate life to your kids and work on growing in those areas. Your example is one of their greatest opportunities to learn how to successfully live this life.

10.

Be the 'Strongly Connected Dad'

Making strong connections with your family makes parenting easier and more enjoyable.

Playing with your kids forms strong bonds.

You can have an amazing relationship with your kids by prioritising forming great connections.

When you can understand, relate to and express love for each other through your daily interactions, your parenting will be much easier and more enjoyable.

Why you want to have a great connection

When there's connection, there is harmony. When people feel understood and cared for, there will be greater peace in your house. Your day-to-day life will be much more enjoyable and you will look forward to seeing your family. Even if your child is going through a tough season, you can still be close by to help, because you are connected. When you have a great connection, your kids are more likely to do what you ask, because they trust that you want the best for them. They feel loved and want to show this love back to you.

The 'Bungee Rope' of strong bonds

Great connection is like a bungee jump rope that flexes under stress and pressure but holds your relationships together. Every time you positively connect with your kids through experiences and interactions, you add another small strand of elastic to your rope. With every new connection moment, the rope grows thicker, adding more strands and eventually, you have a thick rope of great connection. As your kids grow up with the challenges of becoming an adult, the strong bungee rope of connection you have built in your relationship will stand up to the tests and pressures of life. Even though tough times can 'stretch' a relationship, it will stay intact.

Having a great connection makes parenting easier

Forming strong connections with your kids makes parenting much more effective: the words you speak will have more weight, your requests are more likely to be answered, and your life will be more enjoyable. You won't need to guess what's going on in their lives, as you will be more likely to see and perceive what is going on through the relationship that you have.

The kid who was hard to connect with.

Part 1 - The cold shoulder

One of our children was a real challenge to maintain good connection with. We were just not on the same page, in harmony. When they had done something wrong, it would be made worse by their poor reaction while we were trying to parent through the situation, which would often result in a poor reaction from us.

When it was time to be tucked in at night this kid would put up a wall, often grunt and resist a cuddle and kiss. As parents (and humans), the natural response for us was to be disappointed, frustrated, and withdraw. This would weaken our connection and make matters worse. It was like they were testing us: 'Do you still love me even when I act like this?'

Parenting them was not enjoyable. They were not having fun, and there was no connection. We were in a downward spiral.

So what did we do?

Part 2 - The kid who was hard to connect with

After fighting the disappointment and urge to disconnect when hurt, we took a step back to figure out how to get a breakthrough in showing love to them. We decided, we will build strong connections, even if we don't see any noticeable results in the short or medium term. We reasoned that loving this child and rebuilding trust and friendship had to work better than living in this cycle of disappointment and frustration.

So we started a determined love connection campaign with belief statements about the child: 'You are kind', 'You are smart, 'What a great helper.' We would give them a cuddle and kiss and if they resisted we would say, 'that's OK' and not force them. At other less tense times, we would say, 'In our family we say 'Hi' to each other and give a hug'. This established our family's behavioural standards.

We looked at what they did well and encouraged them with incentives to keep going. We thought about what made this kid laugh, and joked in that way. We worked at their love languages and we spent more time on activities that they loved.

Slowly the connection was being rebuilt, and even though there were disappointing set-backs, we just kept focusing on connection. We are still on this journey, but our relationship, connection and life is much better and now we are enjoying parenting them.

What is connection in a relationship?
It's relating and interacting with your kids, where your heart is open to them and their heart is open to you. It's having shared trust and understanding for each other. It looks like two people with arms open, moving toward one another.

Someone once said holding your hands out with palms up helps open yourself up to respect and love for the other person when talking through conflict.

It definitely beats arms folded or clenched fists and at the least being mindful about your approach is a great place to start any relational conversations.

How do you know if you have a good connection?

Ask yourself these questions. Answering with a yes or no will help you define the quality of connection in your relationship:

- Do you look forward to spending time with this child?
- Do your kids come to you when there is a problem?
- Can your kids express themselves to you?
- Do your kids listen to what you say?
- Do you know what is going on in your kids' lives?
- Are you sharing the good times and the bad?
- Are you enjoying your interactions with them and they with you?

How to build strong connections:

Emotionally

Asking questions and talking about what is going on in their life. Listening and understanding is the primary goal before problem solving. Recognising and acknowledging their feelings, 'Wow that must have been hard when...'

Physically

Hugging, smiling at each other, high fives, rumbles. Check out the positive touch chapter 6.

Experientially, doing things together

What do they love doing? Find activities you can do together like games, sport, hobbies, art, going outdoors or reading.

Love languages

Find out what their two primary love languages are, and input into their life in this way. These love languages are quality time, touch, words of affirmation, gifts and acts of service.

Ask where you can help

It may be cleaning their room (together), giving them a ride to their friend's (with a smartphone free drive) or helping with homework.

Giving your belief and confidence
Speak powerful statements, like 'You are a smart kid, I think that you make great decisions'. This communicates trust and confidence in their character. You may be speaking in faith to start off, but words have creative power.

Be connection oriented
When you focus on connection as the goal, life suddenly is full of opportunities to do this.

Compliments and encouragement
Give specific praise: 'Hey, you did a really great job on that piece of art. I love the shading and colours that you have used there.' Your specific insight communicates your interest in them.

Answer their questions well
A question is an invitation for connection. At tea time, when someone asks, 'Dad, how was your day?' Stop what you are doing, make eye contact and give them at least a couple of sentences on what happened and be prepared for more questions. Answering questions well, helps the asker feel valued and that their question was important.

Make time for connection
Turn off distractions: TV, smartphone and computers, which can be easier to connect to than our families.

Forgive and ask for forgiveness
When something has gone wrong, move past being offended and disappointed. Forgive and ask for forgiveness. Talk about what happened and how it could go differently next time, so you learn and move on. This heals broken connections.

How good connection is broken

Not spending enough time together.
Connection relies on time; although if you have to be away, there are ways to maintain connection over distance.

Thinking the worst of the child.
It is up to you to remind yourself daily to look for their potential and all the good that is in them.

Being offended or disappointed at a family member will cause you to withdraw.
Forgiveness is essential to maintaining connection.

Jumping to wrong conclusions.
It's always worth asking 'What happened?' Nobody likes being accused, even less when they are innocent!

Changing your priorities of what is important in life away from connection.
This usually goes from being family focused to 'me' focused.

Where correction happens more often than connection.
You want to make as many good times as possible so that you have good connection when correction is needed.

Practical: Connection questionnaire to create a connection plan.

Your answers to your questions below will help you to create a plan for building your family connections:

What do my kids/wife love doing?

What are their love languages?

What can I ask them about their daily life??

What can we do together that we both enjoy?

What's the number one thing that is preventing connection between us?

What is the last great thing I did that caused a good connection to happen?

What do I positively believe about this child/my spouse? Am I telling them that?

So dads, spend time building strong connections. Creating a strong bungee rope of relationship connection will create a happy fun family that is built to last.

11.

Be the
'Leaves an Amazing Legacy' Dad

Leave a more precious inheritance for your children than money.

Break the cycle.

Your life can encourage, equip and inspire your kids and their kids for years to come. What are the most important things that you want to pass on to them?

What is a legacy? It is something left behind or handed down by a predecessor. You will recognise the beliefs, attitudes and habits you have inherited from your parents. These are part of their legacy to you. Leaving a positive legacy is thinking about and deciding what you do and don't want to pass down to your children. We often think about an inheritance of money as the most important thing that we can leave behind for our families but consider the value of your children inheriting from you:

- Wisdom
- Incredible self belief
- How to help others
- Knowledge of how to have a great family
- How to do something really well
- How to be healthy
- Keys to happiness
- A great work ethic
- Strong faith

Passing on these tools and life skills will set them up for a great life.

One day you will be gone, but your legacy lives on

I know this is a disconcerting thought, but one day you will not be here anymore. However your legacy will, living on through your children and their children. The example to your children of how you lived and what you believed will be replicated, passing from generation to generation like a nugget of gold, silver or concrete passed from old hand to young hand. Whatever you do in this life will continue through your children, and with that sobering thought is the incredible opportunity that you have to choose what your legacy will be.

You can have a massive impact on the world

Sociologists say even the most introverted person affects 1,000 people in their lifetime. Your legacy, the example of how you live your life, in and through your kids lives will impact thousands in their lifetime and 10,000's in their children's lifetime. It's incredible, the impact one person can have! Your attitude to life and your empowerment of others can positively affect the future of tens of thousands.

So what do you want your legacy to be?

Looking back at the end of your life, you will know what the most important things were

I know that when you are on your deathbed, many years from now, you will not be saying 'I wish I spent more time at work; or I wish I read one more social media post or watched just one more Marvel movie (or your favourite tv series)'. You are going to be thinking about the people in your life and how you spent life's moments with them.

Take a minute and picture this end of life moment and what you would be reflecting on as you think about your life.

Write your eulogy now, it will change your life

Have a think now of what you would want your eulogy to say (the paragraph that gets printed about you in a newspaper when you die). This is a brief summary of the effect of your life on the world, and writing down what you want it to say is one of the most powerful things you can do now, to help decide what kind of life you want to live and the legacy you want to leave.

I was really surprised when I wrote down how I wanted to be remembered by those left behind.

It was more like: 'fun loving dad who lifted us to a higher place' than, 'loved watching rugby, sweet lego collection and bought us heaps of stuff'. What would you want yours to say?

Think about the words you would want your kids to say at your funeral:

Dad was a great guy, he worked a lot and we never really saw him but we know he loved us.

Dad spent so much time with us, we had so much fun together and he taught us so much, we wouldn't be who we are today without our dad.

What would you want you eulogy (life remembrance) to say?
Take 10 minutes, think about this and write down how you would like to be remembered. Write your eulogy here:

Two questions to help you identify your legacy

1. What are three things you want to pass on to bless the next generation?

Naturally people want to give money, property and possessions, but what about beliefs, mindsets and emotional skills? What if the number one lesson you passed on was: great self-belief, how to dig deep, how to have a great marriage or wisdom?

Write down what you want to pass on here:

1.

2.

3.

As much as passing on good attitudes and attributes is great, equally as powerful is not passing on the bad or destructive behaviours and mindsets. What are the top three things that you want to stop with you and not be passed on?

1.

2.

3.

Being intentional about your legacy will give you the life that you want now

I just love these deep soul searching questions. Asking and answering them now can save a lifetime of regret. We have the ability to determine what is important to us and start to develop these things in our lives now. For more good ideas ask other people what their three things are that they want to pass on to their kids.

Ask the life veterans

A great source of wisdom is elderly people. Question them on what the most important thing is in life, and those things that they wish they had done, or not done if they could live life over again. They will feel complimented that you would seek their advice.

Older people have lived a lot of the experiences you are about to

Create a life-guiding statement

When you have formed your picture of how you want your life to be with the view of creating a great legacy, write it down and remind yourself of it daily. I love a statement of confession, hung up in a place you see often like your bathroom mirror or your computer screensaver to be read out daily. Your words are powerful, and the words we say create our future.

A life confession statement.

Check out this example of a life-guiding confession statement below. Feel free to take any of this to help to create your own one.

Try reading it out loud now and see how you feel:

- I have an amazing life

- I love my wife and my kids, I am the 'Family First Dad'

- I put my relationship with my wife first and look after my family

- I daily seek connection and to understand my family members

- I have an amazing future which I am planning and preparing for now

- I am a unique individual, like no-one else, I seek to be my best me and don't compare myself to others, I run my race to the best of my ability

- I am great at (write five things here)

- I am great at prioritising, I choose my most important things first

- I love doing fun things that my family and I enjoy

- When I fall, I always get back up again

- I dig deep, I have got incredible resilience and I push through

- My words are powerful, and I speak powerful loving words over my family and myself

- I am a great help, people's lives are better because of me inputting into their lives

- I am thankful for all these things (think of 10 things right now)

- I forgive and move on

- I turn away from negative influences and seek positive education and input

- I have excellent friends who take me to a higher place

- I am a hard worker and do my best in my job

- I am solution focused and am a problem-solver

- I am smart with money and seek ways to educate myself to be better in this area

- I never stop growing, I always keep learning

- I know the love languages of each person in my family and use these to love them effectively

- I hug and kiss my loved ones and let them know how precious they are to me

- I am an incredible dad

- I am a blessing and I will give my kids, family and community a great present and future.

So dads, your life and influence are creating a legacy for your children. I encourage you to live a life that creates a legacy that will lovingly empower thousands of people. Changing your personal world will affect the world.

12.

Be the 'Healthy Device Use' Dad

Raising kids who are in control of their devices and
making healthy choices.

Finding the healthy balance of living in the digital and physical worlds.

Question: At what age should we give our kids something powerful that needs maturity to handle?

A car and firearm is 16 years old and alcohol is 18. (New Zealand, 2022) What should a smartphone or gaming console be?

Cars, firearms, and alcohol have the ability to do great physical damage so the ages closer to adulthood and the training required are justified. But how about devices with less obvious mental and emotional possibilities of risk and damage? What age and training would be safe and prepare our kids for the responsibility of access to the internet, social media and addictive games?

Answer: it's up to you.

Devices are aw..... (fill in the blanks)

Devices are awesome. You can open up your phone or computer and tour anywhere in the world with 3D maps. You can watch the funniest/ most inspiring or crazy things happening in the world. Communication with our friends is instant; a funny thought pops into our heads and 'bam' two seconds later it's shared with them. You can become a fighter pilot, a formula 1 driver or the manager of a professional sports team. You can check out the latest fashion trends happening in Italy. Devices can be awesome, an unlimited world of possibilities just one button click away from taking us anywhere our imagination wants to go.

Devices can also be awful, dangerous, addictive, and waste a whole lot of time. If the world is at our kids' fingertips through devices, so are the scary things in the world. Pornography and violence can be easy for our kids to find or accidentally be exposed to. The games designed for our enjoyment can also be highly addictive. Social media pages are great for sharing our lives but can become an unhealthy source for finding love and value. The ability to be contacted at any time can cause our kids to have no downtime. Faceless communication through texting or public platforms can reduce empathy and to lead mean comments and bullying. Considering all these possibilities, devices can be awful if not used carefully.

So, **Devices are kind of aw.....kward.**

Devices: Getting the best and avoiding the worst.

Who's the boss? Are our families in charge of our devices or are our devices in charge of us? This chapter is about empowering us and our kids to make great choices by weighing up the benefits, understanding what healthy use is, teaching control, and setting boundaries.

We want to have great lives, getting the best of the physical and digital worlds. To live our lives understanding the power for good and bad devices can have. To paraphrase the words of Spider-Man, Peter Parker's Uncle Ben:

'with great device power comes great device responsibility'

Healthy use is the goal.

Devices can be additive and create zombie-like behaviour, they can also be useful, educating, and great for communication. I'm positive we can find a healthy medium of being in control and making smart choices to get the positive benefits while avoiding the negative possibilities. Knowing how to guide our kids towards thoughtful and responsible use is the goal.

Current parenting standards of kids' device use can range from no devices in the house to unlimited and unmonitored device usage. Whatever approach we choose should be made with this thought in mind:

When they are old enough to choose their amount of device use, what will they do?

Think of your kids 2 - 10 years in the future as 18 year olds, with complete choice over the time they spend, what will they choose? The child who never had access might stay up all night catching up on all the TV and gaming they had missed out on in their childhood while the kid who had unlimited use may not know how to be present in an unplugged moment. Our challenge is to help create device understanding and self control to empower our kids to live a healthy life. .

Three factors that can make device use unhealthy.

Habit, Self-Control, Convenience.

Understanding why and how we use devices helps us to see possible usage pitfalls caused by our natural human vulnerabilities. Why is it hard to say 'no' to devices? Why does our use of them often run over time? Why, like a child's cuddly security blanket, do we keep them close? I think the answer lies in these three factors: Habitual use, lack of self-control, and the ease and convenience of close proximity.

Let's call them DUFs (Device Usage Factors, or human traits susceptible to alluring devices). The health test indicators for your device usage, measure your DUFs:

Habit - How often do you find yourself using your device without thinking? (Waiting for something, whip out your phone).

Self-Control - Do you find it hard to stop and often spend way longer than you intended? (Quickly checking the weather turned into 30 minutes of watching YouTube).

Convenience - Are you using your device because it's super handy in your pocket instead of something else that takes more effort to organise? (I could have gone for a bike ride through the forest, but sitting on the couch looking at my phone was much easier).

What all of these DUFs have in common is they are generally unconscious actions and behaviours that we do automatically. So how do we overcome these human predispositions? We make them conscious choices.

Unhealthy device use could be defined as:
'Unconscious behaviours instead of conscious choices.'

Consciously choosing - the secret weapon to put you back in control. 'Hold on, is the best thing to be spending my time on?' When we purposefully engage our families' brains around device usage, we can start weighing the options and making good decisions, which leads to deliberate actions, putting the control back in our hands. How great would it be to teach our kids smart decision-making and develop their strength of character to follow through. To raise adults who make deliberate device use choices that benefit them. For our kids to be in charge of the devices rather than the devices being in charge of them.

'What am I missing out on?' When our kids choose to spend time on devices, what are they choosing to miss out on? We want them to stop and think, 'Is this the best use of my time? Is there something better I could be doing?' or, 'What life experiences am I missing out on by using this device?' Considering what's on offer opens up a world of possibilities to rival device use.

Choosing devices could mean missing out on something way better! Real life is actually amazing (more than we give it credit for). Let's consider these digital vs. real-life scenarios:

Device	VS.	Real Life
Do you want to text your friends,		or go and play basketball, competing, joking laughing, and slapping high fives? (I know this sounds like a 90's movie)
Do you want to play a challenging block game on your phone,		or use your imagination and talents to create a lego masterpiece?
Do you want to watch YouTube's trending videos,		or develop a life skill like drawing or playing your guitar?
Do you want to play a dirt bike game,		or ride an off-road track on a mountain bike or actual dirt bike?
Do you want to scroll other people's highlights on social media,		or climb the closest hill at sunrise, take a dip in the local river, breathe in the views and make your own memories?
Do you want to play a wrestling game,		or wrestle your mates or Dad (always better in real life, until you get an elbow in the groin or end up inadvertently hurting one of the kids)?

Choosing to live in real-life moments also gives us the opportunity to experience present moments like: The sun or wind on your face, the people around you, or the joy of someone laughing. A joke or a smile, the good and sad thoughts and feelings which need to be contemplated and processed. Closing your eyes and taking a deep breath, resting.

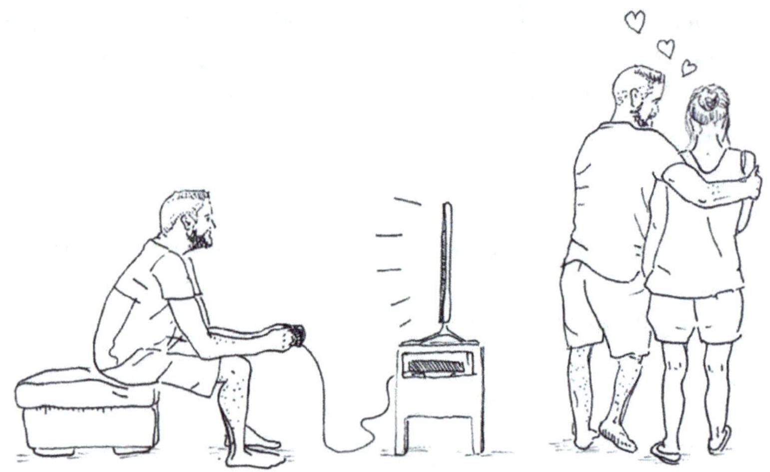

What are we missing out on?

DUF 1:

Beating Habitual Behaviour with conscious choice and device disruption

Using our devices without thinking. We sit down for lunch and pull out our phones. We go to the toilet and pull out our phone. We have a moment's downtime or need to wait for anything and we pull out our phone. Every day we pull out our phones automatically, opening our home screen with our fingers nimbly opening our social media/news page/game/sporting app before our conscious mind has realised what we are doing. It's automatic behaviour. We have repeated this action so many times, it has become a habit. Our brains have formed neural pathways making it easy, automatic, and natural.

Is this bad? Well, if we stop talking to people around us, don't give time to think our life choices through, and choose mind-numbing entertainment over something more substantive, then yes, it can be a real robber of our life's precious moments. When we recognise this habitual behaviour and its unconscious time-wasting implications, we can pause and consider what we could be doing to better spend our time.

Action point: Disrupt your regular routines. Remove the apps that you automatically revert to. Leave your phone behind when you go to the toilet. Taking these 'drastic' measures will jolt your brain from your automatic behaviours and make it easier to not succumb to them. Studies vary on how long it takes to break a habit, but it could be from 14-60 days until you find you are free from some device habits.

DUF 2:

Establishing Self Control by considering and choosing something better.

Devices are like Pineapple Lumps. Saying 'yes' to them could be saying 'no' to something better.

It's hard to say no to Pineapple Lumps; milk chocolate coating around a sweet chewy pineapple centre. They are delicious, tropical with the perfect balance of sugar and taste, addictive.

You open the yellow packaging which separates so easily, revealing the chocolate treasures and before you know it, the freshly opened bag of Pineapple Lumps is a freshly <u>finished</u> bag. You didn't want to eat the whole bag, but these delectable creations were hard to say 'no' to. They are designed to be desirable.

Devices can be like pineapple lumps, once you start, its hard to stop.

Our devices are also designed to be desirable. Social media applications, entertainment, and games are optimised to hold your attention and give you feelings of reward and achievement. Once you start, it's hard to stop.

You can try to not eat the Pineapple Lumps or play on your device, but trying not to do something is often more challenging than aiming to do something else.

Action point: Choosing something better (abs) helps you say no (to flabs).

<u>I love this saying:</u> For lack of vision the people cast off restraint (self-control) - King Solomon (Proverbs 29:18, The Bible). The best way to not do something is to think of something else you would rather be doing and make this your goal. Shift your focus by weighing up what you really want and aiming for that. If the goal is to have a fit body that can do 10 pull-ups and run a fast kilometre, then when you are confronted with tempting Pineapple Lumps, your pre-decided goal helps limit you to 1 instead of 10 (which you enjoy chewing as you walk to the pull-up bar). It's much easier to say 'no' when there is something better to choose from.

DUF 3:

Choosing Substance over Convenience by understanding easy is not often best.

Devices are like a corner dairy or fast food restaurant which is convenient, cheap, and close by. But easy is not always healthy; if you live on what you can get from your local fish and chip shop your health will be very poor. What we consume on our phones and the results we get are very similar to eating fast food. When we consider what we are consuming, it helps us make healthy choices.

Action point: Stop and think about what you are consuming on your phone, is it developing that amazing brain of yours or just entertaining it?

Smartphones are convenient, the perfect shape and weight for our hand to pick up and hold (for a long time), they are always with us, in our pockets, or on the table next to us. They come to the toilet with us, join us in bed, and accompany us to work. The proximity and size make them very convenient to pull out at any time and easily access our digital world. When we understand how easy they are to access and how tempting they are to use because of proximity, we can make decisions to reduce this enticement.

Action point: If the ease of use causes you to over-engage with your device, create separation and identify the triggers to convenient use. I.e., when you are at home, plug your phone in and put it on a shelf, turn notifications off and delete apps you find hard to resist.

DUF conclusion

So with these device usage factors (DUF's, our human traits susceptible to alluring devices) the key to healthy use and being in control of our use of them is consciously considering and choosing what is best for you.

The next step is to create boundaries. This leads us to the dog you just adopted (or already lives with you).

Your Smartphone is a Dog

Lovable and incessant and it wants all your time and affection. Dogs need boundaries (and so do phones)

Every dog owner has decisions to make and boundaries to set. You have just brought a new puppy home, and now you have some important thinking to do about what a dog living with you looks like.
Is the dog allowed on the couch? Can it come inside? Does it sleep in the bed with you?

Is it allowed to jump up on you? These are all important decisions dog owners have to make.

Your smartphone is like a Dog, it wants all your attention.

Dogs, 'man's best friend' are just made like this, it's in their nature. This dog loves you, adores you and wants all of the time you can give it. If it could, it would spend every moment with you, sit on your lap at the table, sit in the passenger seat of your car licking your face and sleep in the bed with you. Who can blame it? They are loyal and love their masters.

This is why we train dogs and give them boundaries, so we get our own personal space, the bed doesn't smell like dog and the house doesn't get hair all through it. If you don't set boundaries, your dog probably owns you more than you own it.

Phone/dog boundaries for us and the kids

Good dog boundaries	Good phone boundaries
No barking at night and school	turn notifications off or shut the phone down
Put it in the kennel for the night	plug it in on the kitchen bench and leave it there
It can't sleep in the bedroom	if you are tempted to check, keep it out of your room
Walk it once a day	set usage timers for social media and time rules for gaming
It can't beg during mealtimes	it stays away from the dinner table
No pooing in the house/ yard	Only add digital friends and followers who will treat you respectfully

Your phone is like a dog. It wants all your attention and needs boundaries. Your phone could be described as your closest companion and 'man's newest best friend'. Just like a dog, it wants all your attention. It will bark (notify/alert) at you all day and night to get you to come and play (use it). It wants to occupy every space you do - work, home, and bed.

It wants to be interacted with, it's been designed like that. The companies who made the applications on it require you to use them to earn money and survive.

If you don't set boundaries, your device could fill every non-sleeping moment of your life. So, do we own our phones or do our phones own us?

Setting Boundaries. If setting boundaries for phone use is hard for adults, how terribly difficult must it be for our kids who are still developing self-control? This is why we need to create boundaries in our own lives and teach our kids how to do this in theirs.

The Babysitter, the Black Hole, and the Band-Aid (being mindful of how we use our devices)

The Cheap On-Call Babysitter...

Devices can be cheap and convenient babysitters, but what parenting/ child development moments are being missed?

<u>'I just need a minute of focus!'</u> We've all been there: we really need to get something done and need focused alone time to do it. The kids are right in your personal space talking to you and you're finding it hard to concentrate. What can give you time alone and distract the kids while you complete this task...? A device! You suddenly have a babysitter that enables you to have a moment of quiet focus.

<u>The downside.</u> Now, this is possibly a great solution, but what can start out as 10-20 minutes can gradually creep into longer times; 30 minutes or 1-2 hours. The downside of this handy babysitter is the same as a real babysitter, which is the babysitter can end up raising our kids instead of us. This can result in kids becoming more addicted to their devices, and us parents missing those moments of raising and developing our kids through parenting or by building relationships.

<u>Using the babysitter cleverly.</u> When you are out of the house in public, for example in a quiet doctor's waiting room, it can be a great moment to use a device to stop your kids from getting bored, agitated, or causing a ruckus. However, this can also be a fantastic moment to teach your children how to work through boredom or to learn to sit quietly. Striking a healthy balance between keeping your kids occupied and parenting could be telling your kids, 'if you: sit still/read a book/do a drawing/ play paper scissors rock/

eye spy or talk to me in a quiet manner for 10 minutes I will give you 5-10 minutes reward time on the device'.

It's important to be mindful of the time and consequences of relying on the device to babysit.

A Black Hole to Consume our Time.

Let's be conscious, not subconscious spenders of our time. Devices can be like a black hole where our time is sucked in and is lost forever. Have you ever sat down for a quick 10-minute browse before bedtime and an hour goes past? You were going to get a nice long sleep but instead, find yourself investigating where the lost squadron of RAF Spitfire Aeroplanes was buried in India in WW2 (you will probably find this in my browser history) and then you can't even remember what you originally opened your phone to do.

Devices can take a huge amount of our time and often don't give an equally beneficial payoff. You go to work and exchange your time and ability for money, your pay. Your time is so valuable that your employer pays you for it and then you carefully choose how to spend the money earned with that time exchange. This is where devices could be accused of being time thieves. They are designed to capture our attention and keep it. A friend likened using his phone to eating a burger that is delicious but never fills you up, so you just keep eating it. It tastes good, but it has no substantial benefit.

Consciously understanding the black hole of time devices can help you stop time loss.

<u>Set a timer.</u> A favourite way of mine to stop unconsciously losing time is this: I decide how much time I want to give my device and set a timer. I do this on my watch, the beeper goes off at the end of the 3/5/10 minute period to alert me the time is up. My concentration is broken, and to continue I have to consciously extend the timer to spend more time. Give it a go next time.

Your time is your and your children's most precious resource, be mindful of the black hole of devices ready to consume a good chunk of it.

When Kids Rely on Devices - a Band-Aid for Life's Boring Moments.

I was recently at a youth event for 11-13 year olds where some kids had devices and others didn't. All of the kids were engaged in the fun moments (except a couple of kids on their phones), but what was really noticeable were the times between the organised fun, when kids had the opportunity to be bored that the phones would come out. The kids who didn't have phones created other fun moments chatted to each other or just sat down watching other people and relaxing. The kids who did have phones pulled them out of their pockets and reverted to their favourite game or movie, and ended up missing out on the spontaneous activity that was being created around them. Their ability to rely on the device for company or entertainment prevented these kids from having to work through awkward moments/boredom/space of time.

<u>Don't Band-Aid what's not broken.</u> Like a crutch is relied on by a person with a broken leg, a device can become a crutch that our kids rely on to deal with life's 'not-fun' or 'boring' moments. However, unlike a broken leg, these moments don't need a nursing aid. They are worth experiencing, as they can be an opportunity for imagination, perseverance or rest. We want our kids to experience these 'down' or 'bored' moments to learn about how to live through them, making the best of each moment.

Social media - what does healthy use look like?

Social media is great for entertainment and seeing what people are doing, but is not a healthy substitute for more communicative relationships. It can also have negative behavioural consequences.

I find it really easy to be negative about social media:

- Looking at other people's greatest moments can lead to comparison
- You are often being exposed to people's intense private opinions
- So many advertisements
- The positive/negative affirming cycle of being rewarded for likes

However there is also the good:

- Connecting with your friends
- Saying nice things to people
- Sharing moments you wouldn't have because of geographical distance
- Organising events

It's kind of like the world around us, if we only focused on the bad aspects of people and society, we would never want to leave home, but there are good aspects too.

It's important to recognise social media is a variation of real life.

The difference is social media was created by computer programmers for you to interact with their application and to sell advertising. These programmes are designed to appeal to what the developers and their computer algorithm (the application's brain) think you want to see (kind of like the way the daily news is a skewed view of the world; bad news sells). They reward you to post content that fulfils their purpose of engagement, which is to get other people's attention and interaction as this makes their site valuable for selling advertising.

The 'like' button was designed so people could say 'cool, I like your post,' but the computer rewards popular posts. So people start chasing 'likes' which can mean creating more extreme posts (controversial content gets lots of attention), or feeling bad if they don't get a good number of 'likes' in response to their post.

This digital reality seems similar to the physical world but can have negative implications, especially with self-esteem and bullying. It's much easier to be mean to someone you can't see than to a person standing in front of you.

The goal is to identify what is healthy and what is not. Social media, when viewed as a part of larger relational connectivity with friends and family, can have healthy aspects. It can also be divisive, comparative and addictive. This can be a struggle for an adult to navigate through. It's even more difficult for our kids who don't have the same life experience and wisdom. Carefully lead your kids and their social media use by making sure it is only a small portion of their relationship makeup.

Tips for healthy social media use:

- Be 'friends' or 'followers' with your kids so you can see all their posts, or have an agreement that you can look at their device.
- Have an age restriction, I think 16-18 is quite reasonable.
- Limit time on social media, this could be 10-15 minutes a day.
- Look at social media together with your children to discuss what other people are posting.
- Discuss what images they post and how things they say can be seen by many people and may be seen on the internet forever.
- Talk about what and when to comment.
- Talk about separating themselves from negative users and 'trolls'.

How to establish healthy device usage:

Be in agreement with your wife about what healthy device use looks like so that you can be a united front in talking about and upholding standards. The questions at the end of this chapter will help you to consider and make decisions on these.

Understand what you are role modeling. The image that you present to your kids every day of how you use your device will be what they think normal device use looks like.

Talk with your kids about healthy phone use. Have a conversation with your kids about the pros and cons, benefits and pitfalls of using devices. You may be surprised at the wisdom and insight they already have. Again, the questions at the end of this chapter will help you with this.

Create a document of agreement for device use with your kids. When you establish a contract of what the privilege of having a phone in your family entails, you are agreeing on boundaries that you can refer back to. It's best to do this before they initially get the device, but it can still be done if they already have it (warn them in advance that you are wanting to look at healthy device use with them).

Set time limits with your kids. This is a great exercise a family member has used with his kids that has worked well: Break the day down together - wake up at 7:00, breakfast at 7:30, leave for school at 8:15, tea time, homework, bedtime, etc. You can then come to a conclusion on how much spare time they have, which leads you to ask this question: How much time do you want to spend on your device? How many minutes do you think is healthy to spend on your device? Break it down to apps/games as well. Come to an agreement, and then set phone time limits. The goal is to give them a realisation of how much (or little) time they have, and what they may be missing out on if their device is their go-to free time activity. You could draw a pie graph of a typical day including sleep, and draw phone time in to give a revelation of time spent.

Understand the device-zombie-mode time frame. How much time is healthy to spend on a device before our kids get apathetic? We have noticed that our kids turn into zombies after about 30 minutes, so we try not to go past that. <u>Set a timer.</u>

Break unhealthy habits by creating good disciplines. If your phone use is out of control on the toilet, don't take it in there. If you are finding you are spending too long on a game, remove the game.

The device is a reward. Devices are a privilege that can be earned through doing tasks and good behaviour. Time can also be taken away through poor behaviour. During the school holidays, we have a chart of tasks that can be completed by earning device time. This gives the kids something to work towards, and you are happy to reward them with device time after seeing all of the positive things they have completed to get there. It's also a great way to establish a work and reward cycle they can use as adults.

Device reward chart (great for school holidays)

Activity	Time minutes	Device minutes earned	Complete
Making a lego creation	30	10	
Reading/drawing or writing	30	10	
Playing outside	30	10	
Helping around the house	20	10	
Play a board game inside or an outside game with siblings	30	10	

Phones have good applications - focus on the positives of applications and devices like podcasts, audiobooks, books, maths applications, find my friends for staying in touch, photography, notes for journaling, and word spelling games. Video chat is a great way to connect with grandparents.

Use actual books, journals, and board games. Giving your kids a physical version of what they are using on their phones can put your mind at ease that they are using their phone correctly (instead of walking past with a worried or accusing statement like 'what are you on...?'). It can also be a joy for them to use something tactile like board game pieces, a pen, and paper.

Monitor and set time device usage with built-in phone device reports. Use the reports within phones to monitor usages - on Apple iPhones, it's called 'Screen Time, and on Androids, 'Digital Wellbeing'. This is where you can monitor usage and set app time limits.

Central home device use areas. Create an area in your house where the kids can use devices where it is easy to see what they are on. It could be easy for your 8-year-old to inadvertently stumble across images or videos when they are mistyping a search on your family computer. Them being aware that you could be looking helps give them more control not to open or look at it.

Monitoring. Check their phone regularly (this is an important part of the contract). Look at their text messages, browser search history, and emails. Praise them for good responsible use and address any concerns.

Understand the addictive nature of device use. This helps you think twice before allowing games like candy crush and also gives compassion when helping to break habits.

Establish social connection times. You can text/talk between these times. Establish connection as a time slot as opposed to constant communication. This works well for our 11-year-old. We give more trust around these times for our 14-year-old, but still monitor.

Notifications - better off than on. Your devices and apps will do whatever they can to get your family's attention. Why? So they can show adverts that add value to their platform or incentivise you to buy more apps or in-game add-ons. Help to protect your attention by turning off notifications and alerts.

Don't use your device for a day. Try stopping for a period of time. This shows us how dependent we are on devices and also what life can be like without them.

Remember the goal: Our job is to teach healthy device responsibility for when they are adults. This is a gradual process of giving them benefits relative to their demonstrated trustworthiness.

Practical: Questions for you and your preteen/teens to answer to establish an agreement:

How much daily smart phone use is too much? How much is too little?

How much social media use is too much? How much is too little?

How much gaming time is too much? How much is too little?

When we are choosing the smart phone what are we saying no to?

How many hours a day should we be available for communication with friends?

What do studies say healthy times on devices are?

How about using social media?

What wisdom about the good and bad of devices do we want to pass on to our kids to make sure their usage is healthy?

How much of our cell phone behaviour is habitual or in control? Could you decide to go without for an hour, a day, or a week?

What are the best things that would happen if we only used our devices for an hour a day? And the worst things?

If smart phone usage is similar to watching TV, should there be key tasks needed to earn time on the device? I.e. job contribution, school work?

If we are going to create a healthy boundaries/usage agreement, what would this look like?

These often include: who pays, what happens if the phone is not used properly, that content on the phone can be checked anytime, healthy daily time frames, and where the phone lives at tea time and bedtime.

The great story of a Mum sharing the unknown dangers
A friend was having a parenting challenge with her 11-year-old daughter getting up late at night and secretly watching online videos. My friend needed a way to communicate the seriousness of the risks and address her sneaking this time.

In the family, there was a 1-year-old baby brother who this older sister would often look after. The older sister was teaching the little boy to listen and obey her requests to stop walking when she asked him so that if he was in a car park he would listen and be safe.

My friend (in a lightning bolt from heaven genius parenting moment) thought and communicated this example to explain and
Here's what she said:

'When you are looking after your brother and tell him to stop doing something, he thinks you are just trying to stop his fun, but you can see all the dangers that he can't. You do this because you wouldn't want anything to happen to him, would you?' Her daughter with tears in her eyes imagining the implications of him not listening or stopping said 'No, I want him to be safe'. My friend then continued, 'When you are watching videos online, you just see the fun of what you are doing, but I see all the dangers and I am trying to keep you safe.'

It was a great moment of realisation for the 11-year-old daughter, impacting her perception and changing her behaviour.

I love our friend's approach because the similarities between the two stories helped her daughter immediately comprehend what her mother was communicating. Our friend's story touched her child's heart and educated her thoughts, which changed her actions.

Dads, you can raise kids who learn self-control and make healthy device choices, who will grow into adults who get the best out of their physical and digital worlds.

It might be a tough challenge considering the heavy and addictive device use in our culture, but I believe their future selves will thank you for your wisdom, guidance, boundaries, and personal example you will lead them with.

Marriage life

13.

Be the 'I Love Mum' Dad

A great relationship with her equals a great family and life.

If the Titanic had not hit the iceberg and Leo and Kate had kids.

A great relationship with your wife = a great family life

When you create a strong loving connection with your wife, you are creating a relationship that will go the distance. The stronger your marriage is, the more happy you will be; finding joy and connection with her in your day-to-day life. This bond of love will be an incredible foundation for your family to be able to meet challenges when they come. Focus on your marriage, make it a priority. You can have an incredible marriage. It is absolutely possible to still be in love with your spouse and enjoy spending time with them 10, 20 or 30 years into your relationship.

Make your love for her the relationship standard your kids will aspire to

You are a role model of how to love in your children's lives. How you treat your wife in front of your kids will be their example of how to love, treat others and the standard of how they should be treated by their spouses.

Complementing, hugging and kissing, listening, encouraging, play fighting, helping out are all positive examples for your children to see.

How do you build a strong and healthy relationship?

Having a healthy relationship at the centre of your family will give your family the best chance of happiness. You will be creating an environment where there are less arguments and hostility, and more peace and love in the home.

If you make an 'in love with your spouse' relationship a primary focus in your life, it will be one of the greatest assets to your parenting!

Throughout their adult lives, your children will gravitate toward what 'normal' was like for them growing up. If you have established the following behaviours as being normal, then you have done them a great service.

Great daily practices to build a strong relationship

- Spend time with your spouse daily
- Talk things through until you can come to a mutual agreement
- Respect each other
- Communicate truthfully (in love)
- Don't try to 'win' by getting one over your spouse
- Seek to understand each other's needs and try to meet them
- Be open to change
- Finding ways to improve
- Find a couple who have been married for a few decades and still like spending time together, and learn from them
- Forgive and let go of past failures
- Don't try to make your spouse more like you
- If you've hit a rough patch in your relationship, don't look for a way out, find a way to make it better
- Play the long game, knowing that there will be ups and downs
- Try to out-give the other person
- Make this relationship a top priority

You don't need to do all of these things everyday. Pick a couple that stand out to you and build a foundation by focusing on those. Small efforts done daily will create a great life time relationship.

10 things that have changed my marriage

Learn about the five love languages. A book by Gary Chapman.

This is very practical and powerful. If you find out how your partner receives love and focus on giving love in those ways, you will have great results! Each person will have two top ways that they feel love from the list below:

- Quality time
- Gifts
- Acts of service
- Words of affirmation (positive, uplifting words)
- Touch

When my wife and I started going out together, I would heap positive words on her because 'words of affirmation' was what I loved receiving. However, as great as my efforts were, I didn't get the expected result of her feeling loved. When we did the 'five love languages' test, it turned out that 'acts of service' and 'quality time' were high on her list and 'words of affirmation' was a zero out of ten (almost completely worthless). After being momentarily gutted at all my wasted effort, I switched to loving her with acts of service and have reaped the rewards ever since!

One of the men that I know was having relationship troubles. I suggested he read the five love languages book. He did, then his wife did, and then he started loving his wife in the 'language' that she would respond to. He came to me one day happily announcing 'I have moved back into home!' I didn't even know he wasn't living there! A few months later he told me 'this book had saved his marriage', amazing.

Why not jump online and do the test together http://www.5lovelanguages. com/profile/couples/

Learn about the love bank - how to build an affair proof marriage.

Here is another great book, full of a revolutionary idea - 'His Needs, Her Needs'. This book has changed my marriage. The premise of this book is that you and your wife have a bank of love on the inside that builds up when you do loving things for each other. Everytime you disappoint her or something as small as leaving the toilet seat up, the bank balance goes down. When you do things that make her feel loved, it goes up.

Positive actions put money in the love bank.

If you keep the love account topped up, you will have a happy loving relationship. Neglect to put love-deposits in, and things start falling to bits. The author, Willard F. Harley gives some great insights into the five top things men and women need to feel loved. The book goes on to look at why affairs occur, and points to when the marital love banks fall into negative, a spouse looks for needs to be met elsewhere. I highly recommend this book.

Negative actions take money out of the love bank.

Maintaining Connection is important.

Don't try to resolve a disagreement if you are not connected. Connection says, 'we can park this issue' while we re-establish trust and love. This also causes a feeling of harmony to reside in the house.

So how do you do that?

- Look to understand where the other person is coming from. Think of how much you love this person, and then love her in her preferred love language to let her know that your relationship is bigger than the problem.

- Let your spouse express emotion without trying to change them.

- If the emotions are too high, say, 'Hey, I love you. We can work on this later or tomorrow. We will work it out.'

- Don't make proving your point the goal.

- Be honest with how you feel.

Learn more about connection in KYLO (Keep your love on) by Danny Silk.

Understand each other's strengths. My brother-in-law resisted his wife's urgings over a two-year period to find their strengths by doing a Gallup strengthsfinder course. Once they did the test, he was the course's greatest fan, shouting its usefulness from the rooftops, and convinced my wife and I to do the course.

A great way of finding your strengths is by taking the Gallop Strengths Finder test, which costs about $30, and is well worth the investment.

This has been amazingly beneficial for my marriage. When you know and understand the key strengths of your partner, you can work really well together. It also helps (contrary to the commonly held belief of men) for you to understand what is going through your wife's mind in particular situations (I'll tell you how in the next chapter).

The next step in building your marriage from the strengthsfinder is looking at getting a Gallup Strength coach, which is more pricey but also very beneficial. A coach will help you understand each other's strengths and how you can use these to compliment your marriage.

Forgiveness. When you stuff up and make a mistake, ask for forgiveness. 'I'm sorry' is so powerful. If you can do it on the day a mistake or offence happened, you will both have a much better sleep that night. Of course you also need to be quick to forgive. Realising that everyone makes mistakes helps increase your compassion. Learn to move on from the offence, not holding onto hurts.

Disappointment and hurt usually come from unmet expectations. That's why it's so important to communicate well. Talk about what is going on in your day; what you are feeling, hoping to achieve and your expectations of your wife. You also need to find out what she is expecting from you, and decide and communicate if you can/want to do those things.

Treat her like a princess and get a princess. Buy flowers, write notes, take her on dates, rub her back, listen to her and value her. There is a fantasy movie called 'Stardust' where a star falls to earth and is revealed as a woman. This star meets a guy and when he loves her, she starts glowing. This is a perfect example of what happens in real life relationships. When you pour love on your wife, she will start glowing on the inside, and people will be able to see her glowing on the outside!

<u>Tip:</u> put reminders on your phone to prompt you to buy flowers or go on a date once a week/month. Even reminders to sit and talk are helpful!

Just an ironic not so subtle swipe at technology preventing meaningful relationship connection, put your phone away on a date.

Live her world for a day. I love the TV programme 'Undercover Boss' where the boss takes a job somewhere in his company as a new employee, but in disguise. The boss experiences life from the employee's point of view, which usually leads to appreciation, and making change in the company.

In the same way, why not live your wife's day to get an appreciation of what she goes through, from beginning to end. Try to do it without her around if possible so that you have to do it all. This has caused me to make major changes in my day, and my appreciation for her has gone through the roof. It's hard pulling together tea, whilst doing the homework while all the kids are hungry and tired. Once you have managed that, after bathing the kids and putting them to bed, just before you feel like sitting down, don't forget to do the washing!

I tried this when my wife was away for three days and it transformed the way I contributed to family life. After living first hand, the tired/hungry 5:00 - 5:30pm meltdown of the kids, I asked for an early leave time from work* to be home 30 mins early. This has been a massive benefit to our family.

*I made up the hours at other times, in case you are thinking your work might not do that for you.

Let her be her. I love the saying, 'when you get married the minister says 'and two shall become one' and then you spend the next 10 years figuring out which one.' Early on in marriage, I remember trying to make my wife more like me, although that wasn't what I was consciously thinking, I just wanted her to think more like me. I stopped one day and thought, 'Why would I want to marry someone just like me?' I wouldn't. You married each other because you were different. Don't try and make her like you or you will lose all of the great differences that make you a more rounded couple. Your differences are usually the areas that you will clash over, so don't look at your spouse as a problem, but look at your relationship as one great whole with complementary strengths. Never forget: the differences are what attracted you to her in the first place.

Prioritise her. Is there any plant more important to water in the garden? Any life area more important to invest your time into? If this relationship fails, to a large degree, your life fails. When you recognise this and spend the time to show love and serve, I guarantee the rest of your life will be better.

Of course, it's still fine and healthy to play sports, hang with friends, watch TV or game, but balance your needs with giving attention to the most important person in your life. You are going to spend the rest of your life with your wife, she is a great investment for your time.

You are on the same team. It's not you versus her, it's you and her. Make this a statement that you say to each other: 'we are on the same team'. This constantly refocuses life's situations and makes it us against the problem, not you versus her.

So dads, pour out love on your wife, and watch your relationship and your family blossom.

Be the 'I Love Mum' Dad.

One more cartoon to illustrate how the love bank works
(which in this cartoon unintentionally looks like an excuse for being a slob).

14.

Be the 'Same Team with Mum' Dad – be a great team

Creating harmony and getting your strengths
and weaknesses working together.

It's good to remember you are on the same team when you encounter conflict.

You and your wife are on the same team.

Although sometimes, it can feel like you are working against each other.
Your spouse might have different family life priorities which are more important to her than they are to you. You could struggle to communicate in a way she understands. One of you thinks fun is the most important thing while the other believes order is what the family most requires. The challenge in every relationship is communicating through differences and learning to work together.

Be greater together. Being a great team is all about getting your strengths working together, understanding each other's weaknesses (or work-ons) and planning and strategising your parenting to agree on a unified course of action. In this 'Team' chapter, I'll share with you how to achieve a team mindset, plus keys on how to become a strong parenting team.

It all starts with you believing 'we are on the same team' ` We are on the same team ' is one of the most powerful statements that my wife and I have started making as a couple. If one of us feels attacked, the other will say 'we're on the same team'.

When you have this mindset, 'we are on the same team', you go from looking after yourself in the relationship to looking after the team. No team can lose when they are united in goals and purpose, and are always looking out for the best for the team.

Sometimes parenting is like tag-team wrestling and Mum needs someone to tap-in

<u>Remind yourself:</u> 'we have the same goals: a loving marriage, to raise great kids and to have a secure and loving household.' It's easy to be offended when you are looking out for yourself, but when team unity is a priority, your mind is geared towards finding unifying solutions.

When you get married, you find someone who has strengths, giftings and attributes that are different from yours. That's because when you join in a relationship with your complementary strengths, you form a very complete whole team.

**Sometimes it feels like you are surrounded and fighting for survival.
Almost like a child zombie apocalypse.**

The apocalypse - what five people would you choose to survive with?
I love this question: if there was an apocalypse, which five people would you choose to have with you, to guarantee the best chances of survival and ensure the continuity of the human race? I always think of gathering as many different experts as possible, diverse in their skill sets; doctor, scientist, construction specialist, biologist and a comedian (to keep everyone sane). The same is true for marriage. If you were to have a child apocalypse, what two experts would you choose? Someone tidy, fun,

disciplined, organised, or spontaneous? You wouldn't want two of the same people, as you would get a very narrow range of skills. You would want experts in a diverse range of abilities. I bet you are thinking right now, 'My wife and I are diverse!'

The power of two - different strengths working together. As a well oiled, fully functioning team you have an amazing opportunity to make much more impact than either of you could separately. As an individual you have strengths and weaknesses. As a couple your strengths will help to cover each other's weaknesses. One of you might be a great planner, while the other is great at doing and completing. One is tidy, the other spontaneous. At first your strengths might frustrate the other person, but when you get your strengths to work in harmony through understanding each other, your differences come to be your greatest strength.

Most of the problems are misunderstandings - team means talk.
'Why did you do that? Why would you act like that? What are you thinking?' We feel like the other person is working against us, and this is where the idea and feeling that we are two individuals in some kind of tug-of-war relationship battle comes from. You are on the same team. Understanding and communication starts to unravel the frustration. As you begin to talk it over, with the goal of connection and 'team', you gain understanding of what the other person thinks, and how and why they act. Be brave enough to be truthful, communicating this in a loving way.

Language to understand each other's strengths and weaknesses.
As mentioned in the previous chapter, Gallup Strengthsfinder has been an amazing source of insight for us in our marriage. It has helped us understand each other's key strengths, what they look like when they are going well and when they aren't. It has been revolutionary. It has given me so much insight into how she thinks and also language for us to use when communicating through 'relational situations'(challenges).

Why not do Gallup Strengthsfinder and coaching with your wife? I strongly recommend it, including paying for the relationship coaching.

Six keys to being a strong parenting team

1. Learning together creates a united approach

Learn together, and discuss parenting styles as you read, or listen to books, podcasts or videos. This way, you are understanding the principles together. When the time comes to put this new technique you have learnt into effect, you are on the same page and in agreement. If one of you is reading and finds something great, make time later in the day to read it to your spouse. Then have a discussion on how this might be implemented in your parenting.

2. Keep your relationship strong

This is one of the most important keys not only in your marriage but in life. There's no point raising great kids only to have your marriage fall to bits. Go on dates, at home and out. Kiss, cuddle and be romantic. As parents, if you only role modelled loving each other really well, it would be one of the greatest lessons you could teach your kids. However, putting into practise great parenting also creates more time and thought space to romance each other!

3a. Be in agreement, united

The kids need to know that Mum and Dad are going to have the same standard. It will give them a sense of peace and consistency. With your spouse, discuss your parenting and come to an agreement on what to do and how to proceed.

How to get in agreement as a couple:

1. Find an issue
2. Discuss the issue
3. Problem solve the issue by seeking advice and getting educated
4. Suggest solutions and then decide on the solution jointly and come up with a plan
5. Follow through with the plan

3b. Be aware of Kid strategies: divide and conquer

Sometimes kids will try this on. If they don't get a satisfactory answer from Mum, they will come to you and vice versa. I have learned to ask 'what did Mum say?'. If their answer doesn't seem right, let them know you are going to need to talk to Mum. You don't need to give them a 'yes' straight away.

4. Get enough sleep

Having a full night's sleep of seven or more hours will refresh you for the challenges of the next day.

5. Manage conflict well

Talk about issues and plans in an energised, rational state of mind. Avoid heavy issue conversations late at night when you are tired. If you feel emotional about something she has said or done, take a breath or a timeout to calm down before talking about it. Often I can misunderstand what she meant when a comment has been made, and misinterpret her intention. Ask questions to understand and clarify intent, 'When you said this... it made me feel like this...'

6. Spend time to plan and debrief

Have a talk at the end of the day. How was your day? What worked? What didn't work? What should we try tomorrow? Life's beautiful gift is that we get a new day every sunrise to implement changes and make small steps towards building a great family.

Dads, you will have a happier, more enjoyable life living in unity with your wife. Keep reminding yourself and saying 'we are on the same team'.

Personal life

"Plenty of people miss their share of happiness. Not because they never found it, but because they didn't stop to enjoy it."
- William Feather

15.

Be the 'Present in the Moment' Dad

Don't miss the moments of joy happening everyday.
Enjoy your life.

What are you giving your attention to?

"Yesterday is history. Tomorrow is a mystery. Today is a gift, which is why they call it the present." – Eleanor Roosevelt

Being present is enjoying what is going on around you and not missing out because of distractions that are less important. Phones ringing, notifications dinging, text messages buzzing for your attention, emails every 20 minutes and the background noise of worries. These are all things that are stealing our present moments everyday. To enjoy our lives we have to pause, look around and appreciate how great life is.

Living in the present moment is one of the hardest challenges that we have as dads. We have got so many things vying for our attention: our phones, TV, work, calls, emails, our friends, hobbies, future dreams and concerns, and of course, our families. Most of these are good things in balance; the problem is that they are usually all vying for our attention at once!

As dads, we have got so many great moments in this life journey to enjoy. This chapter is how to enjoy and not miss them, as well as creating more of them! Let's declutter our mental space.

Not missing out on the good times

Have you ever been driving along the road, started daydreaming and then snapped back to reality and thought, 'I can't even remember driving the last five kilometres!'? You have been on autopilot and missed what was happening right in front of you. This can happen in parenting, and in marriage. Because of the hustle and bustle of family and life, we can just switch on autopilot, be distracted and miss out on the great moments happening around us.

We need to enjoy the years with our kids at home. Kids are so much fun. They help us stay young. Our job is not just to raise responsible, tax-paying citizens. It is also to interact, play and laugh while enjoying the character and personality of these younglings (sorry, Star Wars reference).

The number one thing I have heard parents with grown-up kids who have left home say (with a wistful nostalgic faraway look in their eye) is:

'Enjoy your family while they are growing up, it goes by so fast and they will soon be gone.'

It's amazing how often I hear someone saying this during a week where it feels like I am parenting in a house that is on fire being carried down a mountain by an avalanche (a tough parenting week). Hearing this perspective helps me to take a breath and look with different eyes at my family.

Looking back, these parents acknowledge that even though it was crazy, they miss having their kids around and wish that they had enjoyed it more.

So, here are two keys to really help you enjoy your moments today:

1. **How to be present and give full attention to your family in a moment**
   - Put distractions away - turn off the TV, put your phone on charge.
   - Think how these people are the most precious thing in your life.
   - Look at your family - make eye contact.
   - Think of the things you are thankful for about them.
   - Ask them an open ended question like, 'What was your favourite thing today?' Wait and listen for an answer. Then counter with a question based on their answer, 'How did you feel about that?' or, 'What did you love about that?'.
   - Think and join in with what they love doing: playing with Lego, reading or sports, join in and engage in that activity.
   - Think, if you were in their size 4 shoes: 'What could Dad do in this moment that would be special to me?' Then, do it!
   - Set a reminder to spend 5-10 minutes of quality time every day with each member of your family, it could be a post-it note on your car dashboard.
   - Get 7-9 hours sleep each night.

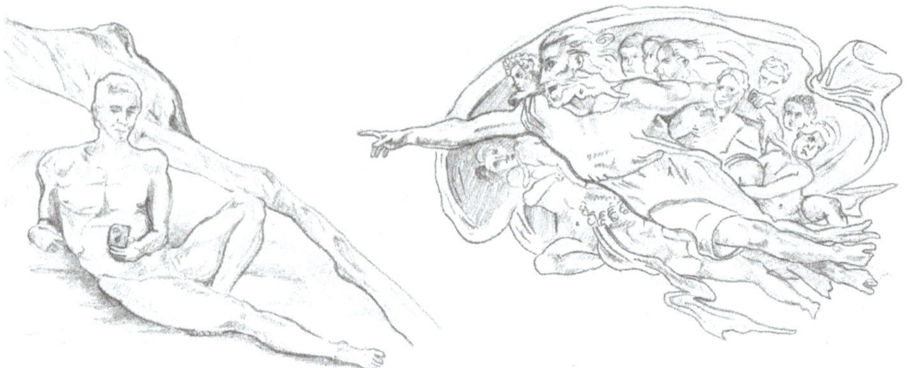

'The Creation of Adam' by Michelangelo might not have occurred
if there had been phones around (it may have only been God reaching out).

2. **Recognising distractions and dealing with them**
   One of the top things stopping us enjoying time with our kids are
   distractions. Our modern culture is full of them, clamouring for our
   time. What is consuming your mind and attention: Smartphones, work,
   worries, tiredness, television...?

Putting distractions in their place:

Devices. They are like a dog that just wants to lick your face. Running
at you, jumping up and demanding your attention. What is it about the
device that takes your attention? Emails, notifications, social media,
phone calls, alerts...
Solution: Here is how to put the device in its place. Emails only during
work time. Have an answering machine. Plug your phone in and give
it a spot to sit in when you are at home. Give social media a special
time of day (tip, delete it off your phone and only view on a desktop
computer).

Put your phone to bed.

Work and work problems - Keep work at work. You only get paid for the time that you are at work, so be really efficient in those hours.
Solution: Put an auto reply on your email outside of work hours: 'I check and answer emails between 9-5pm'. This can be harder with a small business where you need all of the business you can generate, so block out an hour of family time in the morning and evening and rely on the answer machine to manage people's expectations.

Worries - Worries about the future will steal your present moment.
Solution: Write down what you are worried about and one to two ideas on how you will deal with it. When the worried thought comes into your head next, remind yourself that you have possible solutions and will work on it later. Studies have shown that approximately 80% of the things that you worry about will never happen.

Tiredness - Being tired minimises every moment by not being fully awake or aware. Your kids and family get a grouchy zombie to live with, instead of a loving father.
Solution: 'Tomorrow starts tonight', discipline yourself to go to bed at a certain time. Aim for eight hours sleep per night.

Television/online videos - These can suck up hours of your time while you 'numb out' watching them.
Solution: Try going without TV/movies/youtube for a week and have your eyes opened to what a big part it is in your life and how it distracts you from life. Try reading a book, playing a guitar, drawing, exercising or talking to your wife.

So dads, go to war on removing distractions so you can be present and enjoy the moment.

You will enjoy life so much more by putting everything in its place of importance. I'm excited to hear your stories of success. Be the 'Present in the Moment' Dad.

16.

Be the 'Has Enough Time' Dad

Be the Dad with enough time to do what you need and want.

So much to do! (overwhelmed)

'I just don't have any time.'

Have you ever caught yourself saying this? How can you possibly fit everything into your life on top of work and sleep: family, sports and exercise, entertainment, housework, mowing the lawns and personal growth?

I have great news for you. You do have time. We all have the same amount of time - 168 hours every week. We just need to decide what the most important things are to spend it on.

How do you balance all that you need to do with all that you want to do and still have time to Be the Dad? Budget your time. Use your time effectively. Choose what you want to spend your time on. In this chapter I've got five great keys to help you create time for the important things. Plus I've created a time budget sheet for you to help arrange what is most important in your life around what you 'must' do. And because work can take more than its fair share of our time, tips on how to keep work, in work hours. This is how to have maximum effectiveness in your time at work.

What you water with your time will grow

Time is like water to a plant, the more time you pour into something, the more it will grow.

<h2 style="background-color: yellow">Five keys to creating more time for yourself and making the most of your time</h2>

1. **Be time smart**

   You can maximise your time by combining a couple of activities. I want to be fit and receive personal development, so when I exercise, I will listen to podcasts and get both of these priorities in one time slot. You can exercise by riding bikes with your kids, or playing football together. This means fitness and quality time with the kids. On your commute to work, listen to an audiobook (personal development), call a family member or friend (community), or listen to music you love (relaxation).

Be time smart by combining exercise with time in nature and listening to an audiobook.

We need to invest in the areas that will give us maximum benefit, now and in the future. If you could look back at the last 30 years and see what the best investments were in property, the stock market and new technology and go back in time to invest in them, you would be a rich man. <u>With our lives, right now, we can do this.</u> Through the wisdom and experience of others who have lived fulfilling lives, we can know right now what the most important things are for us to focus on and invest our time into, that will give us the best return in 30 years.

<u>Great things to invest your time into:</u>
- Wife - Benefit: daily happiness, love and lifelong friendship
- Children - Benefit: daily happiness, an excellent future for them and lifelong friendships
- Exercise - Benefit: a long and healthy life
- Sleep - Benefit: daily happiness, alertness (according to studies, lack of sleep is the number one cause of depression)
- Work - Benefit: money to keep living, something to feel proud of, skills to grow and develop
- Personal development - Benefit: mental and spiritual well being, a better future
- Community - Benefit: people to love, help, support and be supported loved and helped by others

2. **Being a time smart worker at your job**

   At my work, we employ some excellent mums who have a 4-hour window in their day to work. They are my role models for making the most of time. Mums are time-balancing champions. They have to be, otherwise they wouldn't fit in everything they need to do. They are disciplined and well-planned. When these mums turn up at work, they bring their time management or maximisation skills with them. They know that they have limited time, and I'm convinced that they get six hours worth of work done in four hours.

3. **A balanced approach is the best approach to using your time**

   You may have observed an unbalanced approach in the lives of very successful people in film and sport. They pour so much time into being the best in their careers that they struggle to maintain their family life. I am sure they wish they could have as much available time as we do with our families. Being balanced in your approach to all the areas that need your time will cause each area to grow daily. The short term result might feel like watching grass grow - not that noticeable - but over time, you will have spectacular results.

4. **Save time to do what you love**

   With all of this time efficiency, you can sometimes only leave enough time to do the most necessary things. But one of the most necessary things is being someone who loves life, and is alive in life. Find out what you love (for me this is drawing or going for a run), and put aside time to do this. You will feel happier, rested and more fulfilled.

5. **Identify time-suckers as poor time investments**

   Time suckers are the areas of your life that give little benefit. Social media, television and gaming can be fine in moderation, but in excess will rob you of valuable years of your life. Create time slots for these and develop the self discipline to be able to turn them off when the time allocated is up. Apart from the time wasted on these things, social media can also cause us to wistfully look at the past and worry about the future.

Your Time Budget - Practical

Here is one of the most important things you can do for a great life - budget your time.

A 'Time Budget' that will help you discover what you are spending your time on, and what you can do to free up time for the most important things. You can fill out the table over the page or go online to: www.bethedad.co.nz for a sheet that automatically calculates the totals for you.

With a completed Time Budget, you'll be armed with the knowledge of the available time that you have, and you can tweak your life (and this sheet) by making decisions about what you want to invest your time into.

Our world is full of things fighting for our time and attention. Shut out the distractions that pull you from what is most important - your smartphone, phone calls, emails, auction notifications.

Here is how to create your own time budget:

Fill out the times.

In the table below, fill out column B with the amount of minutes you need for each of the column A activities. Don't limit the time, just enter what you think it needs.

Adding other activities.

In column A activities marked 'other:' fill in other activities that you would like to spend time on, and then in column B, the time you would like to spend on these.

Calculate weekly hours.

Fill in column C, weekly time, by multiplying B, daily time by 7.

Total hours needed.

In box D, add up and total all the results from C. This is the total time needed.

Total remaining hours.

Subtract 168 (hours in a week) from D. this will be a plus or minus figure.

Daily hours left over.

Divide F by 7.

<u>Tip</u> - Once you have created a time budget, guard it.

Your Time Budget

Fill in the yellow cells

Activity	Time needed daily If less than an hour, use .5 to = 30 mins .33 = 20 mins	What that would be per week?
Sleep		
Eating		
Shower, brush teeth, get dressed		
Toilet		
Working	Just fill in the week	
Travel to work	Just fill in the week	
Time with Wife		
Time with Kids		
Playing Sport	Just fill in the week	
Watching TV/ online videos		
Gaming		
Exercise - Running, Gym, Swimming		
Personal development ie reading, prayer, inspirational podcasts, church		
Social media		
Catching up with friends	Just fill in the week	
Chores		
Other		
Other		
	Total hours required	
	Total hours available per week	
	Total hours left over **If this has a minus - then you have run out of time**	
	Spare time left daily (hours)	

Example of a completed time budget

Activity	Time needed daily If less than an hour, use .5 to = 30 mins .33 = 20 mins	What that would be per week?
Sleep	8	56
Eating	1	7
Shower, brush teeth, get dressed	1	7
Toilet	0.75	5.25
Working	Just fill in the week	40
Travel to work	Just fill in the week	3.33
Time with Wife	0.5	3.5
Time with Kids	1	7
Playing Sport	Just fill in the week	
Watching TV/ online videos		0
Gaming	2	14
Exercise - Running, Gym, Swimming	0.75	5.25
Personal development ie reading, prayer, inspirational podcasts, church		0
Social media	0.5	3.5
Catching up with friends	Just fill in the week	0.2
Chores	0.5	3.5
Other		0
Other		0
	Total hours required	155.53
	Total hours available per week	168
	Total hours left over **If this has a minus - then you have run out of time**	12.47
	Spare time left daily (hours)	1.78

Seven keys to keeping work in work hours

Don't let the pursuit of success at work cause you to lose your family and half of all the money you earned. At one of the jobs I worked, there were a number of men in their fifties who had worked really hard, long hours in their twenties and thirties. Sadly, they ended up losing their marriages in the pursuit of success. All that hard work resulted in less time for their relationship and ended up in a marriage split which cost them half of all they earned in the resulting divorce. The way I see it, it would have been better to have worked half as hard, ending up with the same amount of money, but kept their marriage healthy and seen their kids every day.

1. Put a limit on it.
If you are at work for 40 hours of paid time, limit it to that. I can hear the protests now, 'But I won't be able to get my work done in that time!' It's OK, I have been there. Hear me out: Starting from next week, write down in order of priority all of the tasks that you have to do and then how much time you have to do them. It will probably be longer than your 40 hours so you need to get smart. If you are a salary worker, aim to get all of your jobs done in or under a 40-hour week; depending on your remuneration package, every hour over this, you are working for free.

2. Do a time budget for work.
For the tasks that you have to do in your work day and week.

3. Plan your day.
Write a list and prioritise important tasks and allocate time to completing these. Add in 1-2 hours for distractions/unplanned urgent jobs.
I recommend reading The One Minute Manager by Kenneth H. Blanchard and Spencer Johnson; a story about being efficient at work.

4.   Plan tomorrow at the end of today.

You will have a very clear sense of your priorities.

5.   Your first two hours are your most effective.

Put your most important tasks here - usually not emails. Put jobs that energise you into the low energy times of your day, typically 11-12 in the morning and mid or late afternoon.

6.   Necessity is the mother of all invention.

Only having a set time to do everything will cause you to come up with genius ideas to work smarter and harder. Write shorter emails. Use technology to make jobs faster. Think of time-saving systems.

7.   Innovate with your time - working like a mum.

Plan like you only have four hours in your work day to get all your jobs done, you will come up with great innovative ideas to make it happen. This is working smart. We employ mums who can only come to work for 4-5 hours a day but get 100% productivity squeezed into that time. How? They are efficient planners and workers as the mum of their family working to fit everything into a limited amount of time. They have a time cap, so they are great at time management and making sure that no moment is wasted.

And if you still can't fit all your work into your work hours...

Ask your boss for help. Let your boss know about your time struggles and how you want to create a healthy life balance. A happy, healthy worker who does their best in work hours is a great worker. Happy workers are a pleasure to work with, are more likely to have creative solutions, and create a great team environment. Your boss hopefully, probably knows this. Reach out and ask your boss for help if you have tried your genius ideas, and your work can't be done in the paid time available. And finally,

Home time is home time. Only answer work emails and phone calls in work time - Put an auto-reply on the email, a voicemail on the phone and leave work at work. It can be this simple. There are exceptions like real estate agents and business owners but in those cases, you will have or need to create other downtimes in the morning or middle of the day for family time.

**Think of ways to get the most out of your normal work hours
so you don't have to work after hours.**

*So guys, this can be difficult to budget out our
time, but it is worth it.*

**It really helps you appreciate and choose wisely what to
spend your time on. Managing your time will help you be the
Dad with enough time on his hands.**

17.

Be the 'Joyful' Dad – find your joy

Finding your joy is a source of strength and important in enjoying your life and family.

Find your joy

Finding your joy.

"Don't ask what the world needs. Ask what makes you come alive, and go do it. Because what the world needs is people who have come alive." - Howard Thurman

> **joy** *noun*
>
> 1. *a feeling of great happiness, 2. a source or cause of great happiness: something or someone that gives joy to someone*

OXFORD LANGUAGES

Guys, finding your joy can bring you to life! Joy can be a major source of strength, energy and excitement and an important key in enjoying your life and family. Finding Joy is all about discovering and doing the things you enjoy! It is also about effectively reducing areas that are 'joy-killers'. So let's create a great foundation of joy in your life!

Your Joy and excitement is a great sustainable energy source for your family. The Bible says, 'The good man out of the abundance of his heart brings forth good things.' When you have joy on the inside, it will overflow into the people around you. This can be one of a dad's key roles in his family; bringing excitement, imagination, joy and energy into each day.

You being full of joy (joyful) is a win/win for you and your family. You are enjoying life, and your family are enjoying you.

Firstly you need to find or rediscover your sources of Joy. What is it you love to do that you feel excited about and enjoy? Most likely, it's activities that energise and fulfill you, like: hobbies, using your talents, being your unique personality and character, the outdoors and other activities.

Dig deep to find your Joy - it takes effort. We dads can get into a cycle of work, eat, sleep, repeat, where we are just going through life on autopilot. When we get into this cycle and are dog tired at the end of the day, we can look to 'numb out'. 'Numbing out' is looking for escapes which take our mind off our busy lives: TV, video games, social media, etc. These escapes can be fine in moderation, but doing activities that bring you joy will energise you! We can feel too tired to get out and engage in an activity that requires just a little more effort but doing so has big rewards. With these activities you come alive, find more joy and life becomes more interesting!

Find your unique-ness. I love the scene in the movie 'You, Me and Dupree' where fun-loving, manchild Dupree inspires his worried and life-tired friend, Carl, to find his "ness". Dupree says "Man, you are Carl, where is your Carl-ness?" (Where is the thing that brings you alive!?) Search it up on Youtube!

When I start sinking into this place of tiredness and worry, my wife says to me 'where has your "Ferg-ness" gone'.

So guys, where do you find your 'ness' (your Joy)?

Thinking about what you do have - Thankfulness and Gratitude

Pause for a moment right now and think of three things that you are thankful for and why. Taking time when you wake up or go to sleep to be thankful for three things can help you appreciate your life. This actively fills your mind with thoughts of joy, which can take the place of negative thoughts. When we are thankful, we realise our lives are much better than we thought.

Future bringers of Joy that you haven't even discovered yet! There are activities you don't even know you will love until you get out there and try them! I love painting, and I only discovered that recently! Painting slows me down, focuses my mind, and gives me so much pleasure having created something. What could be your undiscovered thing?

Great ideas to find your Joy:

Be you, your unique personality and character - weird, funny, imaginative, caring, serious or inspiring. It is easier to be your unique character working in your strengths than trying to 'fit in'. You may really like 'dad jokes', bless the world with them!

I love drawing in nature - Roys Peak, Wanaka

<u>The arts</u> - music, poetry, painting, sketching, spoken word, dancing. I am a terrible rapper but I love it. You don't need to be good at the thing you do, as long as you enjoy it. The goal is not to sign a record deal or sell paintings, it is to have fun!

<u>Sport</u> - shooting hoops, tennis, cycling, rugby, cricket, paintball, airsoft, etc. And you don't even need to be good at it, sports are for having fun.

<u>Exercise</u> - walking, bike riding, swimming, running, kayaking, paddle boarding. Doing exercise produces happy chemicals - endorphins.

<u>Hobbies</u> - Lego, modelling, radio control cars/planes.

<u>Culture</u> - going to cafes, art or music events, museums, admiring architecture, visiting libraries and live sports games.

<u>Experiences</u> - visiting new places, exploring, trying a new thing, animals, meeting new people, riding the bus or hiking.

<u>Helping others</u> - giving, coaching, teaching, leading your local scout group, helping at your church. Also a great example of serving and commitment for your kids to observe.

<u>Education and internal growth</u> - read/listen to books and podcasts, study, learn about history, develop your inner life. Daily prayer time really helps set me up for the day.

Factor a time into your day or week to go to try something new or to do what you love. If possible, take your family too.

The family that plays together, stays together.

What brings you alive, that you can bring your kids along on?

Here's some examples of my friends who do what they love with their kids.

Digger Dad: A good friend loves diggers. He has access to diggers and trucks in the business he is part of. He can go with his boys to a farm and drive them, doing projects. His nine, seven and four year old boys go with him and play in the dirt, and join in on the activity. I have no doubt that at some point in the future, his passion will become their passion and they will become heavy machinery operators.

Skater Dad: My brother-in-law loves skateboarding and the skatepark. Guess what? His kids love it now too; learning how to skate, scooter and ride with him in the park. When they get home, all faces are sweaty and beaming.

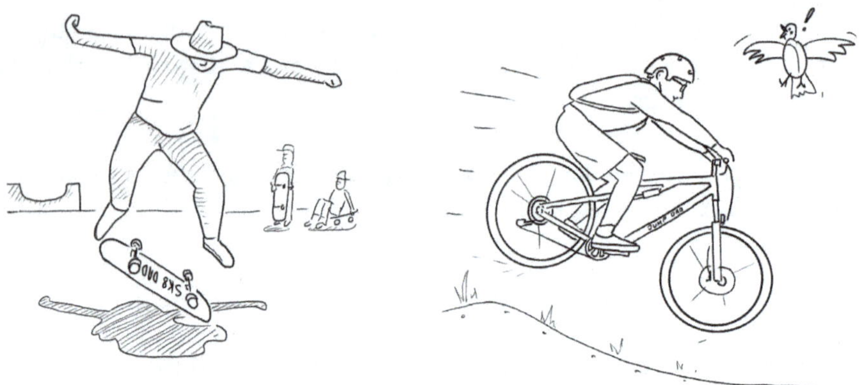

Mountain Biker Dad: I have another friend who loves off-road mountain biking every other weekend. He takes his family into the outdoors and they all ride, jump and skid their bikes, sharing the joy together.

Have more Joy by reducing 'joy-killers'..

Joy-killers are areas that can prevent you from being joyful in your life. They can use up your precious energy and time. So here are some Joy-killers and how to beat them:

<u>Worry</u> - write down your concerns instead of continually pondering them. Spend time planning and educating yourself on how to best handle them if they are upcoming events.

<u>Lack of sleep</u> - be disciplined to get 7-9 hours per night. When you are tired, it's hard to enjoy anything and it's easy to be the grinch that stole the family fun.

<u>The news</u> - reduce your time spent watching it. It's mainly shocking or concerning, and doesn't make you feel greater about the world. Plus, most of it is outside of your control.

<u>Negative friends</u> - encourage or talk to them about being positive, or create distance and find positive friends.

<u>Regretting the past</u> - Don't let dwelling on the past steal present moments. The past is gone, however the present moment is yours to live in, and enjoy and all those to come.

<u>A poor relationship with your spouse</u> - Don't settle for a lukewarm marriage, look for ways to make it great! Read books, seek help, and make time to make this relationship better.

Plan to enjoy future moments
I have a friend who would work hard right up until the night of Christmas Eve, and then on what should be one of the most joyful days of the year, find himself sitting next to the tree on Christmas morning in a stunned, half awake state with his hoodie over his head, still in his boxer shorts.

After a few years of this, he said to himself, 'this is the best day of the year, this is not how I want to spend the day', 'I want to bring the best version of myself'. So he planned all of what he needed to do to be fresh on this 'best day of the year'; finish work, wrap presents a week early, go to bed early on Christmas Eve, wake up and have a shower early.

When this last Christmas morning dawned, he had carried out his cunning plan, and he was able to be the fun, engaging dad that his kids and wife preferred, over the boxer short, hoodie wearing sad guy in the corner. He loved the day.

Don't miss your moments

Don't miss your opportunities for Joy

A family friend, who was a very hard worker and also wealthy, was diagnosed with cancer and sadly died in his fifties. His reflective words of wisdom towards the end of his life were: I am envious of the normal working-class family who have the weekend off and go boating and bike riding. Our friend would work massive hours, at nights and on weekends, working towards a financially prosperous tomorrow. When his life was unexpectedly cut short by cancer, sadly he'd missed out on so many past opportunities of having fun and enjoying life with his wife and kids.

So dads, find your joy, seek out what makes you come alive, those things that electrify the blood pumping through your veins and take your Family along on the ride to Be the 'Joyful' Dad.

18.

Be the 'Enjoy the Journey' Dad.

Success is a journey, not a destination.

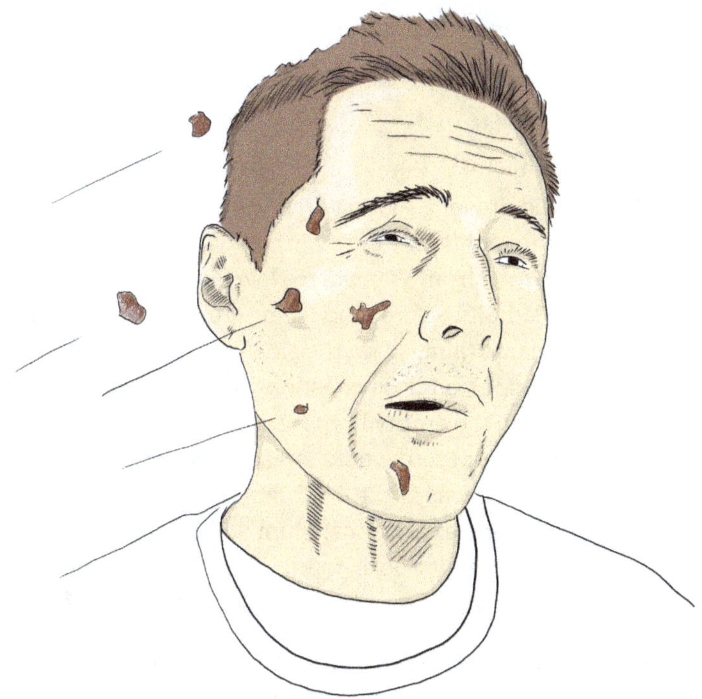

Poo in the face.

'Success is a journey, not a destination.
The doing is often more important than the outcome.'
- Arthur Ashe

Q: Is parenting enduring or enjoying? A: It's both.

Our parenting and relationships are like taking a lengthy journey. In sports its called playing 'the long game' where you faithfully and diligently do many small things to get to your goal. The largest percentage of our lives is spent on the way to where we are going, not at the destination. Realising this can change your expectation from trying to reach a goal, to enjoying the moments along the way.

So, here is how to enjoy the journey of raising a family in the crazy hustle and bustle of our lives, including how to enjoy every day, and ways to make each day fun.

I'm excited about the change in mindset you could experience after reading this!

The never ending van ride

I'm sure my Mum would dread the long van rides (Mitsubishi L300 1984, then 1988, Google it) that our family of seven would take. A two-day-long haul of 15 hours on the road from Wanaka to New Plymouth with no air conditioning and no iPads. Kids throwing up, fighting, my brother and I playing the dead arm game (hint, sit on the side where your strong arm is away from the other person), endless questions of 'how long' and the real possibility of Dad pushing the empty light too far and running out of petrol. I could imagine that my poor Mum would look out the window, heave a long sigh, and wish that she was at the destination. However, instead of it being a never-ending painful experience, Mum and Dad would make the trip fun for us with stories, audiobooks, family songs, I Spy games, rotating front seat turns, numerous stops, lolly bags and food. Mum made it fun.

Sometimes though despite her best efforts, someone would throw up, and with that sickly smell filling the van, it was hard to enjoy, although it did give us something to make jokes about.

**Our families L300 Mitsi Van, I swore I would never own a van
(we have an estima which is only 80% a van)**

To endure or enjoy?

Our lives are like this long van ride. We can view it as a monotonous task to endure in order to get to a destination, or we can enjoy the journey and create special moments on the way.

The great news is that it is up to us to choose which perspective we want to take. The choice of enjoying or enduring the journey of parenting is yours to make.

Your kids are going to poop on you, have a laugh.

When we were potty training our eldest daughter, I got caught with a "Number Two" (a poo) in the underpants. Not mine, hers. 'No big deal' I thought with a genius plan coming to mind, 'I will hold her over the bath and take the pants off'. Any fall out would be in the bath, which would be easy to clean. The plan was going well with me holding her above the bath with one hand and trying to take the undies off with the other hand, until the undies got down to about knee height. She looked down, saw this big brown intruder in her pants and panicked. A cry of 'yahhhhhh!!' burst out from her mouth and she started running in the air, literally running, kicking to get the undies off. The result; a poo sprinkler. It was actually amazing to behold, and it happened in slow motion in front of my eyes. Poo was flying everywhere, all over the bathroom, towels, the basin, the walls, and all over me. I couldn't decide what was more amazing, the artistic patterns, or the even coverage of poo around the bathroom. It was a laugh or cry moment. The clean up would take ages! I took a moment, still holding her above the bath and I thought, 'At least this didn't happen to her mum,' (it wouldn't have, she wouldn't have risked it all to take a shortcut) and then 'I'll look back on this and laugh'. Plus 'What can I do? It's already happened'. So I started laughing and called my wife in. She was amazed and started taking photos (just joking). I made sure to let her know that I would clean it up (poo is my thing). The poo really was everywhere and the novelty would definitely have worn off if it wasn't for the slow motion image of the poo sprinkler playing on repeat in my mind.

<u>NOTE:</u> This is definitely not how I respond every time, but it's worth taking the win and trying to learn from it.

The poo sprinkler, rapid and unequalled in its poo distribution

So prepare yourself, adjust your expectations about this being a growth journey and take it day by day...

Your kids will get it wrong and you will get it wrong.

Days will be both hectic and feel never ending. You are going to need to repeat the same messages and phrases of direction and guidance over and over, thousands of times; wash your hands, say thank you, close the door, treat others the way you want to be treated. You will fail to feel like a winner some days. You will plan, attempt the plan, adjust the plan and then try again. You will go through this cycle over and over throughout a 20-year plus cycle. There will be tears, joy, relationship problems, relationship solutions and obstacles that you will overcome and push through until one day, the kids are fully grown. And if you focus on the people and not the tasks, you will be sad to see them leave.

Captain Shackleton turned a freezing marooning on Antarctica into a fun experience

Plan to enjoy and see the gold on the way through

Most of the greatest stories are about overcoming struggles and hardships. The Endurance Ship's captain Ernest Shackleton was marooned on Antarctica in the early 1900's, with his crew in the freezing winter cold, his wooden vessel being slowly crushed by the ice. The crew could have just shivered, given up, frozen, and perished, but Ernest gave them activities like reading, drama and games to keep spirits high through this tough winter experience. The crew and Shackleton survived with the credit given to the captain for his ingenuity in making the best of the time. Parenting is not as dramatic as being stuck on the ice through a harsh Antarctic winter, but like Shackleton, we can not just endure but choose to enjoy, so here are:

10 keys to enjoying your family life journey daily

1.   Thankfulness helps you enjoy the journey.
When the kid wets the bed and you are changing the sheets, you can let it get you down, or try being thankful that:

- (a)   you have a kid
- (b)   they have a bed to sleep on
- (c)   you have a washing machine and sheets to wash
- (d)   you all have a roof over your head
- (e)   one day your children will be through this stage.

Thankfulness gives you joy in hard moments.

Thinking of what you are thankful for

## 2.	Learn from the day before

Don't get discouraged, learn from every experience and set yourself up for success next time. For instance, from last night's 3:00am bed wetting incident, I learnt what to do next time: I need a spare set of sheets ready. I need a 'wet the bed blanket protector.' I need to take the child to the toilet before bed. I could wake the child up to go to the toilet when I go to bed. I need to not give them a massive glass of water before bed! Learning from the past can make next time better!

## 3.	Write down the wins

Journal the special moments. Think back over your children's witty comments, the unusual insights and the surprises. We were watching a documentary on lions hunting their prey with my then five-year-old son, who made an insightful comment to which I remarked how impressed I was that he knew a fact about lions. He confidently replied, 'I actually know a lot about Africa Dad.' Classic.

Self proclaimed five year old lion expert

## 4.	Celebrate milestones

Celebrate milestones, make it a family party. Potty training, starting school, tying shoe laces. Stop the family and have an announcement: 'Ladies and Gentlemen, on this special occasion we honour and knight Sir <insert your child's name> for completing their first chapter book.'

When our young 2 year olds finish their morning breakfast, we love to hoist both their arms skyward and cheer '<insert your child's name> is the winner, the champion, yay!!!' They look around, relishing the fun, smiles and attention. Positive affirmation for doing something great for their age. We don't actually say 'insert child's name', that is for you to imagine how much fun it will be to do in your family. Go on, give it a go.

For our kids struggling to eat their meal a celebration made reaching the goal worthwhile

5.   Have a goal, a destination that you are heading for - refer to Chapter 2, Be 'the Dad with a Dream'.
Plan to succeed, just like a journey. Figure out the destination early and set a plan for how to get there, i.e. to have fun and laughter raising your kids by making more jokes.

6.   Laugh or cry - you have a choice.
Poo all over the bathroom. Stop, take a moment, look around and picture this moment in the grand scheme of your life. When you put it in perspective, the small moments don't seem as big as they feel in the moment.

7.   Appreciation - smell the roses

Stop in the middle of doing the dishes and look at the people around you.
They are your people, your tribe. Think about what is special about each of
them and how far they have come. Appreciation makes the colours seem
brighter, and the moments more special on your journey.

Pause, reflect and appreciate your family moments

8.   Take a minute at the start of the day to consider:

What is important for me and my family today?
How do we effectively get through the day?
How will I make Mum and the kids feel special and loved today?
What can we do better than yesterday?
What can we do to make this day a little special?
What is the word of wisdom or inspiration for me to take into this day?

9.   Find others on the same journey

Find other families travelling on the same journey, at the same stage, with
similar values and goals with whom you can share stories and experiences.
Encourage other parents and be encouraged; you can learn from and
support one another. You can find these families at pre-school, school,
sports, scouts, guides, work, interest groups and church.

On the Prisoner of War death marches in the Pacific Theatre in World War 2, the allied prisoners held captive by the Japanese would physically support and encourage each other, and as a result, more people survived to reach the destination.

10. Be unique as a family and resist comparison
Different families have different goals and values. Facebook and social media platforms can be an unrealistic highlight reel with which to compare your progress. People generally share the best photo, not the one where everyone was screaming a moment before. Everyone has their own struggles. Figure out what is important to you, what comes naturally, works for you and live like that.

Enjoy the journey

A Tour de France cyclist who had competed in many races retired. He returned to the old courses which wound through beautiful and breathtaking scenery he had previously ridden on to ride them again non-competitively. This time he remarked what beautiful scenery he had missed appreciating due to speeding towards the finish line. Let's enjoy the journey and not just speed towards the finish line.

12 easy ways to make the day fun:

1. Pick a daily mundane experience and make it fun by making it a game

2. Dance while making breakfast

3. Put on an audiobook in the car

4. At tea time, ask the kids what the favourite thing in their day was

5. Dry them out of the shower using a different countries style every night (make it up by using accents and a national anthem)

6. Put undies on your head when you say goodnight

7. Make faces on the plate with their food when you dish up

8. Make tidying up a race

9. Get your imagination involved

10. Talk in a different accent

11. Ask everyone to make up or tell their favourite joke at tea time

12. Have an impromptu cuddle rumble - a wrestle without fists and people getting hurt

This life is your journey Dads, enjoy it, and make it one to remember.

19.

Be 'Daducated' – get wisdom through education

How learning to learn will improve your life.

Reading a book is like having a conversation with the author, in this case Winston Churchill.

You don't know what you don't know. What you don't know could hugely improve your life.

Gaining wisdom and learning more about parenting, living a healthy life and relationships will give you some of your greatest life rewards. Forget university for this, I'm not aware of a tertiary three year course of how to be a healthy Dad and husband. Just put the learning keys below into practice and your family will hand you your diploma of quality living, good times and laughter.

The Dad diploma, not officially recognised outside of this book, but probably one of the most legitimate qualifications you can get.

The educated man who needed education

<u>I opened this book with a part of this story, here is a little more background:</u>
I sat on a flight from Wellington to Christchurch next to a highly educated young father. He was an important part of planning for the infrastructure of New Zealand's future. He shared his plans and how it would benefit the country. A really smart guy. We then started talking about relationships, parenting and mental health. He opened up about how he was struggling in each area. It was great he was so open, and I got to talk with him about great ways to help in each area, to help build the infrastructure of his

personal life. At the end of the flight after saying goodbye and wishing him well, I walked down the boarding ramp and onto the airport tarmac excited for him, and it struck me that our educational priorities and endeavours are primarily focused towards our jobs. We don't realise there is a massive knowledge void in our personal lives.

It's amazing, we get a university education or intensive job training to learn to do our jobs, because it is important to our future to do these right. But with parenting and relationships we just turn up on day one, hoping to instinctively know what to do. If there are two areas in our lives that can bring us the greatest reward or heartbreak, it would be these two.

Your educational investment into your marriage and parenting will not only benefit you and your family, but many others around you.

Here are 11 keys to start educating yourself on parenting and relationships:

1. Realise that learning will give you benefits straight away
As soon as you have learned a parenting principle, it will start benefiting you in your day-to-day life. I remember the day when my father-in-law asked me, 'How many times do you want to ask her to come before she comes?' regarding my repeated asking of our first child of three years old to 'come'. This made me think. Of course, 'once' was the answer, but it wasn't until I learnt from him that I didn't have to ask three times or raise my voice, that this was a possibility. I now have five kids, and I can't imagine how much accumulated time and frustration this has saved over all these years.

Tip: Read the simple process to do this in the 'Wins, Lessons and Discipline Dad' chapter under 'Eight keys to change and train good behaviour' - Getting the kids to do it the first time.

2. Better to learn from someone else's mistakes - someone has walked this journey before you.
I love this, you can either learn from your mistakes or from other people's mistakes (and victories). It can take a lot of time and effort, trial and error to figure out a parenting plan of action and how to put it into effect in your kid's life. Learning from other people saves you so much wasted time and

energy. Be a genius and pick up the tips of people who have learnt the lessons before you. These people love sharing a tip that would have helped them.

3.   Get a picture of how good parenting and relationships can be
When you read other people's stories it can open your eyes to the fact that:
- Kids can obey the first time
- Kids can help around the house
- Kids can be nice to each other
- You can have amazing friendships and fun times in your family

Just knowing that there is a better life and possibility for your family gives you hope, and the dream of reaching that place. Knowing what is possible is the start of the journey of change.

4.   Set aside time to be educated
When you see value in something, you invest your time into it. Your quality relationship with your spouse and the future of your family will be as good as your input into them. I encourage you to set aside time to read or listen to parenting books or podcasts. Start with 5 minutes a day and increase from there. Listen in your car on your way into work. Follow people with great parenting advice on social media. Subscribe to 'the parenting place' informational emails.

Your future you will thank you for your investment in education.

5.   Education forms the culture/ethos of your parenting
Establish what kind of dad you want to be, and then look at how you will try to achieve that. When you start parenting, you have a basic idea of what kind of parent you want to be; maybe a fun dad, life coach, wise sage or professional sportskid creator. It's usually a blend of how you were or weren't raised, plus ideals of what you would like your family to be like. However, when life starts getting busy and you have less time and energy, you have to decide what is important and what principles or parenting ideals you hold onto or let go of. Reading about other people's principles and the things important to their parenting gives you a great idea of what to develop in your family culture.

Time spent reading results in learning great and helpful things

6.   Spot the gaps. What are you struggling with? Study that.

When you recognise an issue in your parenting or child's life, it can be a gift. This insight shows you an area that you need to work on and gain education in. Once you have researched and found a good solution and applied it, your quality of living increases. Also Google can be a great source of information (just check it's from a good source) try searching: 'how to get kids to listen to you' and see what comes up.

7.   Education prepares you in advance

If you have filled up your mind with parenting advice, when a challenging situation arises, you are likely to be much more prepared to handle it, as you have created a 'bank' of knowledge and advice. Often you have listened to someone else's story, and have some good options stored up and ready to use. It's like having a multi-tool with many different tools that you can unfold and use.

'Success occurs when preparation meets opportunity.' - Zig Ziglar

The more parenting and relationship stories you read and listen to the more resources you have to draw on.

8.   Learn together as a couple

It is so important to be on the same page with your partner in parenting, there is much more power in a combined approach. It's great to talk about your suggested solutions with your wife before putting your plan into action so that you are united. I have had many times putting a plan into action without telling my wife and she looks across the kitchen with a quizzical look on her face and she's thinking 'what's this new parenting technique?' Read and learn together, discuss the principles and concepts, how you feel about them and how you will put them into effect. Sometimes planning is done on the fly like Mr and Mrs Smith in the self-titled movie, crouching in the garden shed quickly planning how to battle the 100 agents waiting outside (except you are in the laundry brainstorming and no-one has a hit out on you).

9.   Learn from mistakes

Wins and lessons. If a situation doesn't work out right, do what every good sporting team does, go away and review what happened, and what could have worked better. Look at your approach, go back to a favourite parenting book for fresh ideas and try again.

10. It takes time - realise that you will accumulate knowledge and experience

At the start, it can feel like you don't know much, but you have time on your side. Thankfully when your wife gives birth, it's not to a 15-year-old, yikes! You will start to build a foundation of parenting principles, and then lessons and experiences will build on top of these. This knowledge discovered and implemented will start accumulating and create a core culture of behaviour in your family: listening, respect, love, kindness. Also as your older kids grow, they will help educate your younger kids: 'in our family we do this'.

11. Find great parenting role models

It's great learning from reading and listening, but it's hard to beat learning from observation.

Find a family that is respectful of each other, whose kids listen, where you can see love between the parents and family members and spend time with them. Ask questions, ask for advice.

Find mentors - ask your parents questions, talk to older parents in your community who have good relationships with their kids. Great questions can lead to insightful conversations: 'How did you get your kids to go to bed on time?'

So dads, go for it, commit yourself to living a life of investment in learning, and Be the 'Daducated' Dad.

Notes:

Great methods to learn

- Read Parenting books
- Follow Social media feeds from Parenting experts
- Sign up to email subscriptions from parenting experts like NZ's The Parenting Place.
- Listen to podcasts and audiobooks on parenting and relationships.
- Watch YouTube parenting videos
- Observe other parents
- Experience: wins and lessons, what worked, what didn't

Great resources:

- Danny Silk, Loving Your Kids on Purpose.
- NZ Authors, Ian and Mary Grant books - The Parenting Place.

20.

Be the 'Growing' Dad – your personal growth

Have a better life by investing into your personal growth.

Water your inner man.

If you want to be an amazing dad and man, and have a great life, invest into your personal growth. The changes that happen on the inside when you invest into your heart and mind will powerfully impact every area of your life.

'The good man, out of the treasure of his heart, brings forth good things.' – Jesus

What you feed your mind and spirit will lift you up or pull you down.

My friend who battled to change his life

I have a great friend whose name is Michael. Michael's life was going okay. He had a fairly good job, enjoyed hanging out with his friends, loved playing sports, and had a fairly stable relationship. And then he heard the greatest news, he and his partner were expecting a daughter! Something changed in Michael, he got a vision of how he wanted his future life to be. He wanted to be different, better, happier. Michael set out to make changes in his life to match the new vision he had. He changed his music to songs with more encouragement, he started listening to audiobooks which educated and encouraged him and he became more selective about friends. He even started spending money to meet with a life coach to deal with past hurts and to work on his strengths and weaknesses. Michael never looked back and now eleven years later, you would not recognise my friend today, compared to his former self. He is happy, confident and inspirational! He is an incredible dad of five children, and everything changed because he made a decision to focus on personal growth.

So how do you achieve personal growth?

Firstly you need **motivation**, a desire for **change**. For Michael it was the upcoming arrival of his daughter. Then you need a **picture of the goal** that you want to grow toward and **plan** how to get there. He wanted to be a great father for her. Then you need to start and **take steps each day** towards reaching your goal. He immediately changed what he was listening to. Lastly, you need to **not give up.**

The following are keys that will give you great personal growth.

Goals and how to reach them - three key steps.
A goal is a picture of how you want life to be. Spend time thinking about what is important to you, choose the best two to three ideas and use the following process to get there:

1. **What is the vision/goal?**
   How do you want your life to be?

2. **How and how long?**
   Figure out the steps you will take to get there and set a reasonable timeframe.

3. **Daily steps.**
   Everyday do small actions that will move you towards those goals.

Here's an example...

1. What is the vision/goal?
To be someone who is an encourager to others using positive words.

2. How?
Every day: Think of three great things about each of the people in your life. Look in the mirror and say 3 encouraging things to yourself. Listen to encouraging podcasts on the way to work. Separate yourself from negative friends.

How long?
Do the above plan over 12 weeks, 'I will know I have improved because people will start feeling better around me, possibly saying 'thanks for saying that' and it will become easier to think of positive things about people.

3. Daily steps.
Write this goal and the steps you need to take and hang it upon your bathroom mirror. Do the steps from point 2 daily. Diary/journal down the wins and progress you experience as you grow.

Change

Seeking to grow towards a great future will inspire personal change and doing small things everyday will get you there. Change is like a tree growing, almost imperceptible but can be clearly seen over time.

Eight keys to personal growth:

Moving on from past hurt and disappointments so they don't steal your future.

<u>Forgiving and moving on from past hurts.</u> This can be hard, it doesn't mean that what happened to you was OK, but forgiving starts freeing you from the person who hurt you and the past event. You may need to forgive over and over, every time you think of what happened. It can help to engage with counsellors and psychiatrists, there is no shame in this, it's smart, like going to the doctor when you have an injury - which this is, an inner life injury.

Here is a phrase you can say out loud that can help; 'I forgive (insert name here) for past hurt, I leave it in the past, learning any lessons I can without forming a hard heart, and move into a greater future.'

<u>Apologising.</u> It might be that you were the person who caused pain. Asking for forgiveness can help you and those you wronged move on.

<u>Forgiving yourself.</u> Often, we blame ourselves for things that have been done or have happened to us. As much as we need to forgive others who were involved, we might also need to forgive ourselves if we had a part to play. If you have apologised, made amends or changed your behaviour, don't let past guilt hold you back from positive future change.

<u>Learn and move on.</u> Treat the past as 'wins and lessons'. Learn from past failures and move on. Replace past hurt with future success. I love the Robert Kiyosaki quote, 'Winners fail until they succeed,' and as John Maxwell says, 'fail forward'.

Finding good people to spend time around - Friends and Mentors.

<u>Find good friends whose lifestyle will inspire you to grow.</u> When you can observe people who have great relationships, have a good work/ life balance and are successful in their parenting, you are inspired and educated to grow. We have found that spending time with a happy

family who may have kids older than our own is great for observing and modelling our life on. As you look for the good, also separate yourself from negative or mediocre friends with whom it may be more comfortable to spend time, but will not inspire you to grow. This saying is true: 'show me your friends and I will show you your future'.

<u>Find a mentor to help give you guidance and wisdom.</u> An older person who has an interest in your well being and has learnt lessons from having lived through the same stages of life can give you great advice. A mentor observing your life can have a perspective that you may not have been able to see yourself. This mentor could be a parent, relative, or older person whom you respect and trust. These relationships can be formal where you arrange times to catch up or informal phone calls and conversations when needed. We have found that our local church contains some really great 'next generation' parents who are happy to help us. Alternatively, look for mentors at work, sports clubs, or public clubs like the Rotary or Lions clubs. Taking time to find a mentor whom you can ask for help quickly pays off as their wisdom applied is more advantageous than learning by trial and error (and way less messy).

The wheel of balance - a self check exercise

The wheel of balance is an exercise where you rate how much time and attention important areas of your life are given: sleep, exercise, family, work, input, drinking, entertainment, etc.

I have guided many people through filling out their own wheel of balance, and there is almost always one or two areas that become apparent to work on, and once improved or balanced has produced great personal results.

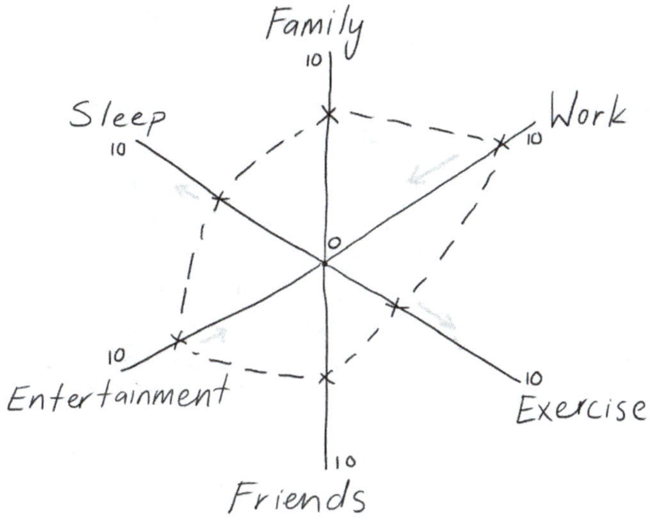

The Wheel of Balance, a simple exercise to figure out what areas you need to give more or less time and attention to for better life balance. (Recommendations in grey)

How to fill out your own wheel of balance:

1. Draw the spokes of a wheel radiating out from the central 'hub' and then rate one (towards the centre) to 10 (end of the line) how much time or energy each life area is given.

2. You then draw a line connecting these points creating your wheel. If there are big spokes and little spokes then when you draw a line connecting these it becomes apparent the wheel of your life won't run smoothly if it was made to rotate like a wheel. This shows areas that are being given too much time or are lacking in time or effort.

3. Conclude which areas need more or less time spent. With the pictured chart, work could have less time with personal development and family time needing more.

This chart has been amazing for me personally, and I often use it for reference.

You are what you eat - personal input and the difference between Inspiration and entertainment

What you feed your mind with is what you think about, and our thoughts steer our actions. If you read motivational quotes at the start of the day instead of news headlines, you are more likely to head off to work in a more positive frame of mind. The benefit seems obvious, but it is challenging to make the choice between entertainment and inspiration. On your way to work, you can listen to the radio and be entertained by funny hosts or you could arrive at work having just listened to a story from inspirational speaker Tony Robbins that could change your life forever.

Most TV, movies and music won't help you get to the place you want to grow to. Don't just ask, 'is this good for me?' but ask 'is this inspiring me and helping move me forward to where I need to be?'

Important note: steer clear of these things which are guaranteed trouble: Porn, gossip, too much negative news and agitated content on social media.

So just like we put good, clean, hi-octane petrol in our cars, let's feed our minds good fuel.

Sometimes the drive to work is great for thinking things over, other times a great opportunity to hear something that could improve your day

Identify growth inhibitors (negative things that stop your growing)

These are things like watching TV, buying things, comfort food and alcohol that we turn to when we are hurting or to escape the world. Some of these can be healthy distractions to help us recharge and are fine in moderation, or they can become negative addictions we start relying on. It's important that these temporary bandaids, which make you feel good for a moment, don't stop us addressing an issue that needs a solution. If we turn to them often they can become addictive habits that are hard to break.

Here are some questions that will help you identify outlets that are healthy or the start of a negative addiction:

- What do you do to feel better when life is hard?

- Is the benefit of this good for you in the long term?

- Does doing this help you grow into a healthy person mentally, physically and with healthy relationships?

- Could you stop if you wanted to?

An example of a healthy distraction might be watching sports highlights for 15 mins a day. An unhealthy addictive version of this could be watching with no time limit and the need to check in multiple times a day.

Quantity, repetition/how often and the power to stop are factors that differentiate between something being healthy and an addiction.

Keys to overcoming negative addictions:
Find something to replace it with: positive confession, exercise, reading or listening to inspirational material.

Set yourself a goal of going without it, to break the habit. Start small and build up; 1 minute, 10 mins, 30 mins, 1 hour, 1 day, 1 week, 1 month.

Separate yourself from whatever you have identified to be a negative influence. Don't buy your favourite chips, or only buy one bag a week.

Let your partner and a trusted family member or friend know what you are going through and aim to overcome. Allow them to help journey with you in overcoming this.

Hit up the key emotions that lead you to turn to this thing. What is the internal feeling that triggers this? Get to the root of this issue and look for solutions, i.e. I just need some excitement, I feel trapped, I'm bored, there is no hope.

Know that you have the ability to overcome it.

Identify your strengths and weaknesses and work on them

What could I be great at? What comes naturally to me? These are your God-given talents that you know or are yet to discover. Work on and develop those things. There are a lot of personal development resources available online.

What are my weaknesses? How can I grow in these areas? What can I learn to overcome them? For example, I was a messy kid growing up, and would lose things which really frustrated my father, as it was a waste of our family's money. What helped me was Dad giving me mantras like, 'don't put it down, put it away.' This really helped me to improve in this area.

Write down your top three strengths and weaknesses and put next to each a couple of 'work-ons' to improve these.

Be OK with change taking time

In the music industry they say that an overnight success is 20 years in the making. A big reason that we give up is that we don't feel like we are making progress. Have confidence in doing the right things that will produce the right results, and understand that it takes time for a seed to turn into a tree.

Don't try to be perfect. There is no such thing. Just be better than yesterday or last week. Be honest with your family, 'Hey kids, Dad

is working on this, it's something that I am growing to be better at'.
You will be able to look back over 3-6 months and see your progress.
Personal development takes time.

Don't compare yourself with others.

Don't compare your growth to someone else's growth. They will find
some areas easier than you to master and vica versa. The only person
you can control is you so focus on your growth and what you can
do to make it happen. If you want to measure progress, set realistic
measurable goals and check your progress against these.

So dads, start by dreaming about how great life can be,
then plan and start moving towards a great future.
Go for it dad. Be the 'Growing' Dad.

21.

Be the 'Family First' Dad

Put work and distractions in their place so you can enjoy your family.

Leave work at the front door.

You are in a world fighting for your time and attention.
Here is why and how to put your family first.

What is the most important thing to you?

Your dirt bike will get old and rust, your friends will come and go, your video game will get hacked (like mine did in 'Call of Duty') and you will lose your hard-earned profile, the important sports games you watch will fade into a memory, your work will continue day in and out, your big hard earned muscles may fade and droop (I hope not), but the most important thing that you will ever have is your family gathered around your deathbed and all the memories you have shared with them.

Life is competing with your family for your attention.

Money, success, fame, hobbies, news, sports and entertainment are all competing with your family for your focus. What you value is what you prioritise. I believe you will not look back at the end of your life and regret putting your family first.

If you put your family at the top of your priority list you will:

Have a happier marriage. Have happier children. Raise children who are more prepared for adulthood. Make many more memories. Enjoy your day more. Possibly make less money. Play less video games. Watch less TV. Let your boss down more (depending on the boss). Spend less time with your friends. If you are happy to agree to those terms, sign below (just kidding), read on how to proactively put your family first.

Nine ways to put your family first:

1.   Make a commitment to have a great family.

When you got married, you made a commitment to your spouse: 'I am going to love you and stick with you through good times and bad.' Your priority: a healthy marriage.

When you have kids you make the same decision but without the formality of the wedding ceremony. Maybe we need the formality of an official occasion like a wedding, so that we make a conscious decision on what the most important thing is. Raising happy and healthy kids in a great family is now your goal.

When it comes to deciding what to do this weekend and it's between your number one fun activity or your number one commitment, your family - what will you choose? Your commitment to have a great family will help you decide. (Note, this is not saying that you don't have any fun weekends away from family - see number 2 and 9.)

2.   How to put your family first without resenting them - balance

All the areas of your life are like plants, they need time (water) and love (sun) to grow. Going to ride your dirt bike or doing your favourite activity are not inherently good or bad. It's in the context of how they fit into the rest of your life. Consider:

<u>Scenario 1.</u> After a balanced week of work and home time, you have just spent Saturday with your kids, working around the house and having time with them in the afternoon, you then having quality time with your wife in the evening. Sunday morning you get up and have breakfast with your family and then go on your pre-planned dirt bike afternoon. You are home in the evening to tuck them in and say good night. TICK, win for the family, win for you.

<u>Scenario 2.</u> You have worked late all week and not been around to have tea with the family or help put them into bed. Saturday comes around and you sleep in because you are so tired. You watch sports on the couch in the afternoon and then a movie at night. The next morning you have breakfast with the family and announce you are leaving for the day to go riding.

BANHHH (negative buzzer sound), win for you, fail for the family.

The difference was the balance of your time investment to your family during the week. In Scenario 1, the love tanks are full. In Scenario 2, the love tanks are empty (and the rubbish bins are full). You need to find the balance in your life where your and your family's needs can be fulfilled.

3.   Plan and Prioritise.

At the beginning of the week, make a plan of all the things you need to do to make sure that everything gets time in order of priority. This will enable you to decide what comes first and then how to fit in the other things that you need or want to do. Refer to the Time Budget in the 'Be the enough time Dad' Chapter 15 to help you do this.

A great guiding question is:
What time investments can I make to get the best returns?'

4.   Accepting that being a dad is paying a price.

You probably have friends with no kids, less kids or who just spend time differently to you. Imagine you are out at a friend's family BBQ and are watching a really great sports game, and there is only 10 minutes left on the game clock. You are enjoying it and really want to see the end but, you have already stretched your wife and kids that extra 10 minutes past when you needed to leave to get them into bed. You have a tough decision to make. Do you stay late with your kids who are getting more tired and enjoy this tight ending, or do you leave, miss the end of the game, but have a more rested family for tomorrow and avoid a disconnection with your wife? The choice comes down to one thing - you. You have the option to pay the price to make your family the most important thing, and they, and more specifically your wife, need to know that they matter the most.

<u>Tip</u>: Be smart, think ahead, anticipate the game that you want to watch. Plan with your wife if and how you can make it happen.

It's about changing the mindset from 'me' to 'us.'

5.   Why 'us' is the best way to look at your life.
Being a giver is the key to having an 'us' family culture instead of a 'me' culture. When you give, the other person is receiving joy and love, and you are experiencing joy at giving. When you look at the world through a 'me' mindset, you will never have enough, no one will be able to keep you happy. When you role model giving, your family will watch, copy and reciprocate. Looking at the world through an 'us' mindset will always seek to make others happy, and in doing so become happy yourself.

6.   Putting work in its place - see Chapter 16, 'Be the enough time Dad' for a list of tips.
Work is an important necessity to provide for our families, but discipline is needed to manage a healthy work/life balance where work doesn't overtake the rest of your life.
I love this saying from fiercemarriage.com: 'Men, never let overworking steal quality time from your family. They would rather live with you in a tent than without you in a mansion.'

We work to provide, but making money is not the only important thing we provide as a dad.

Sometimes we can give our all to our work and have nothing left for home

Work will take as much time as you can give it. If you give work your afterhours, answer your emails 24/7 and keep your phone switched on all the time, the emails will keep rolling in and the phone will keep ringing. So what do you do to keep work in its place? You get your work done in work time. It's better to work half the hours, earn half the money and keep your family, than work twice the hours and lose your family and half of all you earned when your wife leaves.

7.   Tomorrow starts tonight - get sleep.

Putting your family first is having enough energy and alertness provided by a good sleep to have your best self present. 7-9 hours of sleep is very important. One of the leading causes of depression is lack of sleep. You are much more likely to be grumpy and make bad decisions when you are tired. In WW1, the opposing armies camped in the trenches on the western front knew this and would fire artillery shells over at constant intervals to sleep deprive the other side. When I have had a good sleep I am not just present, but engaged and I don't feel like I am in the trenches.

8.   Give your family time.

One of the easiest ways to tell your family that they are the most important thing in your life is to give them your most important resource - time. Plan time into your day to spend with them.

9.   But not all your time.

You could read this chapter and never do anything for you again. This chapter is about viewing your priorities and placing family above work, sports, entertainment, not never doing those things, but understanding their relative importance. For you to be a great Dad you need to get away, be alone and have fun with your friends, because doing these things contributes to your happiness. Wisely consider the needs of your family and yourself to maintain a healthy balance.

So dads, putting your family first can be tough, but it starts with a decision, that your family is more important than work, your projects, hobbies or friends.

Once you have that decided, all of the other choices in life become a lot easier. It's a decision you may need to make everyday but I know you will never regret putting them first.

Be the 'Family First' Dad.

Bonus Round

Have Fun, Be Your Best You

Get comfortable and enjoy being yourself on this life's journey.

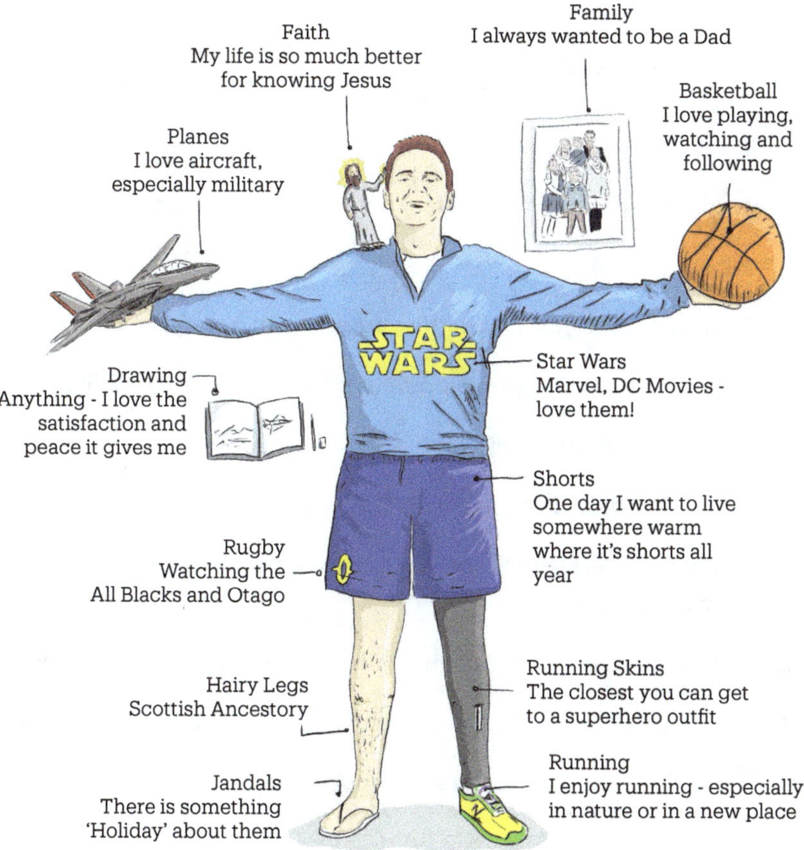

Who I am.

Find your sweet spot of being yourself, having fun and continuing to grow as a Dad.

There is no perfect dad, but there is being the best version of you. The most natural way to do this is blending what you learn about life with who you are. It's easier using your personal strengths and traits in your parenting than trying to be like someone else, plus it's a lot more enjoyable. You will try your best, and some days it will work, and sometimes it won't. Just never give up. Being 'The Dad' is a journey of always seeking to be better. So how do you find that sweet spot, the natural balance of being you, having fun and continuing to grow in your relationships and parenting?

Here are 11 ways to be your best version of a dad:

1. Have fun and be yourself

2. Understand there is no perfect dad, only human dads

3. Never give up

4. Don't compare yourself to the glimpses you get of other dads

5. Realise your dad life development continues your whole life

6. Kids are a blessing, enjoy them

7. Find other dads to be real with and be real with them

8. Recognise the life seasons you are in i.e. new baby, kids sports, teenage connection

9. Keep it simple, choose a couple of work-ons and major in these

10. Ask yourself, what does winning as a dad look like?

11. What does not winning as a dad look like?

1.   Have fun and be you

Do you know how blessed you are to be alive and reading this? Life is a gift, we can take it too seriously and miss out on the fun. Who are you? What jokes come naturally to you? What do you like doing? How do you show love? Have fun and create fun, may your kids and wife say, 'Dad brought us fun'.

Are you different from others? Everyone is, people just hide their true self to 'fit in'. Embrace being an individual, no one was meant to be the same as anyone else. Have fun and be you.

2.   Understand there is no perfect dad, only human dads

I can't do everything in this book all the time, but I can aim to do my best with what I know all the time. The goal is not being perfect, but growing.

Life is a race against yourself.

This is not a race against other dads, it is a race of who you are, against who you can be

3.   Never give up

Never give up, if you get knocked down, keep getting up and taking positive steps forward, every step takes you closer to the life you want to have. When you get discouraged, grit your teeth, look at your vision and re-familiarise with the steps you need to get there. Remember, change takes time. If you consistently do the right things, success will come. Winning is waking up everyday and deciding you will do your best even if yesterday was awful.

I love this quote from Winston Churchill, the man who guided Britain through some of its darkest days in WW2 and on to victory: "Success consists of going from failure to failure without loss of enthusiasm."
And this one, also from Churchill, the last quote my grandfather Des told me "Never, never, never give up".

4.   Don't compare yourself to the glimpses you get of others
It's almost impossible to look at someone else's life and understand what their life is really like. We only see the surface, yet we compare ourselves to this incomplete image. Social media is where we view other people's lives. The moments seen are usually their highlight reel; the happy family at the great holiday destination doing something amazing. It's really easy to look at these images and feel like you are not doing well, but what you don't know is if an argument had broken out just before or after this photo. The same goes for when you see families in public. WW3 could have taken place in the car minutes before, and now the couple is smiling and everyone is behaving. We don't know what their life is really like. Everyone struggles, argues and has bad days, don't compare yourself to what you think another family is like to measure your progress.

5.   Realise your personal growth continues your whole life.
It's like how they would build a massive church in the old days, it would take a generation, 30, 40 or 50 years, but every day the building would slowly become more of a complete structure. Your life is that epic structure. You lay down a foundation of the most important things: loving your wife, loving the kids, understanding what type of family you want to have. Then you lay down some bricks of learning how to show your love to them, the love languages and making these relationships strong. You lay and re-lay these bricks a couple of times, figuring out how to get these fitting together the best. Then you put up some walls of being present, getting educated on parenting and discipline.
And on and on, day by day, until the building gets bigger and bigger as you keep coming back to the foundation, the walls and the roof, tweaking them, adding on and making them stronger. Your commitment to growth will keep you growing.

Like building a monument takes days, weeks and years so to does building and developing your habits, characters and behaviours (this picture is your effort building your life).

6. Kids are a blessing, enjoy them

Don't get so caught up in parenting and providing for your kids that you miss the joy of being with them. Their energy, imagination, optimism and clear eyes are an elixir to your soul. Enjoy your life with kids, it doesn't last forever, even though it can feel like it.

7. Find other dads to be real with and be real with them

Find good friends that you can trust and confide in. Being 'The Dad' is not being the tough guy who pridefully battles alone. I am part of a group of dads that we call the 'tight 5' (a rugby scrum reference). We video call one morning a week and each of us has a turn sharing our struggles and triumphs. There is much laughter, advice and wisdom and then we pray for each other. None of us likes missing a 'tight 5' morning, as this time of fellowship makes us all stronger.

Find a group of dads you can share your struggles and feelings with. As you open up, it will empower them to as well. Sharing the burdens with trusted friends who can listen and offer good advice makes these burdens a lot lighter. You are then pushing forward as a team and not as solo men. Hearing their struggles gives you a more complete picture of being a dad and smashes through the façades that we judge others by. Sharing with trusted friends takes us out of isolation, and creates an unstoppable band of brothers.

8. Recognise the life seasons you are in

Recognise that some seasons of parenting and life are harder than others. An example is pregnancy, and the first three months to a year of a new child's life. When you take a step back and look at your total life, you realise this is just for a period of time. In these trying times, you need to trust in the process of getting good sleep, positive daily input, exercising, practising the love languages and digging deep.

If you are in a tough season in your marriage, keep going and put time into; giving, listening, quality time and forgiving. Also, reach out for help. We have seen marriages on the brink of breakup who did these things and now they are more in love than ever. Enjoy the good seasons and when hard seasons come, brace yourself, lean into the wind and keep going.

9. Keep it simple, choose a couple of work-ons and major in these

Choose one or two things to work on in your parenting and relationships, and focus on these. Be like the basketball player who wants to raise their free throw shooting percentage. They choose this one area to improve on, and put the hard work in at the gym, shooting hoops from the foul line, until they master this area.

Take this same approach, focus on the area to work-on daily until you get the breakthrough. Sometimes this has been one week or one year, but it always improves.

10. Ask yourself, what does winning as a dad look like?
Keep coming back to what you want to achieve. Is it:

- Trying new things
- Being yourself
- Having fun
- Loving your family and being there for them
- Always seeking growth and wisdom for yourself and your family
- Finding a community for your family of safe uplifting people
- Doing your job to the best of your ability and always finding ways to add value to yourself and your work
- Sharing your emotions with trusted people
- Looking after your health so that you can be around for a long time
- Forgiving
- Speaking words of life over your family

11. What does winning as a dad <u>not</u> look like?
Release yourself from the burden of:

- Being perfect
- Getting it right all the time
- Comparing yourself to other dads
- Doing every parenting technique
- Going alone

So dads, thanks for taking the time to invest in yourself to be a better dad, husband and to have a better life.

**Take every day as it comes, never give up, do your best and
I know that you will succeed at being 'The Dad'.**

About Ferg

I am a 42-year-old father of five. I am married to an incredible woman
and mother, Amy and we have been married for 17 years. I grew
up in Wanaka, in the South Island of New Zealand and now live in
Christchurch. I love many things but drawing, motivating others and
leadership are high on the list. Amy and I are family leaders in our local
church and we want to see people have great marriages, enjoy and
excel in parenting and have great mental and emotional health. We
believe that practical life skills education will make daily and family life
much more bearable and enjoyable. I am on a journey of learning how
to be a great dad, husband and man, and hope that this book helps you
in your journey.

Eva, Oli, Amy, Theo, Me, Charlotte, Soph

Great resources to learn more about parenting and relationships:

Loving Your Kids on Purpose, Danny Silk

Growing Great Families , Ian and Mary Grant
Growing Great Boys, Ian and Mary Grant
Growing Great Girls, Ian and Mary Grant

His Needs, Her Needs - How to build an affair proof marriage, Willard.F. Harley

The Five Love Languages, Gary Chapman

Have a new kid by Friday, Kevin Leman

Parenting your powerful child, Kevin Leman

www.ingramcontent.com/pod-product-compliance
Lightning Source LLC
Chambersburg PA
CBHW071606030726
47593CB00001BA/340